THE
KINGDOM
OF CHILDHOOD

[XXI]

FOUNDATIONS OF WALDORF EDUCATION

RUDOLF STEINER

THE
KINGDOM
OF
CHILDHOOD

Seven Lectures and Answers to Questions

Given in Torquay, August 12–20, 1924

Anthroposophic Press

The publisher wishes to acknowledge the inspiration
and support of Connie and Robert Dulaney

❖ ❖ ❖

Original Translation by Helen Fox ©1982 Rudolf Steiner Press
Revised Translation © 1995 Anthroposophic Press

This volume is a translation of *Die Kunst des Erziehens aus dem Erfassen der Menschenwesenheit*, which is volume 311 of the Complete Centenary Edition of the works of Rudolf Steiner, published by Rudolf Steiner Verlag, Dornach, Switzerland.

Published by Anthroposophic Press
www.anthropress.org

Library of Congress Cataloging-in-Publication Data
Steiner, Rudolf, 1861–1925.
    [Kunst des Erziehens aus dem Erfassen der Menschenwesenheit. English]
    The kingdom of childhood : seven lectures and answers to
questions given in Torquay, August 12–20, 1924 / Rudolf Steiner.
— Rev. translation.
        p. cm. — (Foundations of Waldorf education : 21)
    Includes index.
    ISBN 0-88010-402-3 (pbk.)
    1. Waldorf method of education.   2. Anthroposophy.   3. Education–
Philosophy.   I. Title.   II. Series.
LB1029.W34S7313
371.3'9—dc20   95-12247
                        CIP

CONTENTS

ABOUT THE TRANSCRIPTS
OF LECTURES

The results of my anthroposophical work are, first, the books available to the general public; secondly, a great number of lecture courses, originally regarded as private publications and sold only to members of the Theosophical (later Anthroposophical) Society. The courses consist of more or less accurate notes taken at my lectures, which for lack of time I have not been able to correct. I would have preferred the spoken word to remain the spoken word. But the members wished to have the courses printed for private circulation. Thus they came into existence. Had I been able to correct them the restriction *for members only* would have been unnecessary from the beginning. As it is, the restriction was dropped more than a year ago.

In my autobiography it is especially necessary to say a word about how my books for the general public on the one hand, and the privately printed courses on the other, belong within what I elaborated as Anthroposophy.

Someone who wishes to trace my inner struggle and effort to present Anthroposophy in a way that is suitable for present-day consciousness must do so through the writings published for general distribution. In these I define my position in relation to the philosophical striving of the present. They contain what to my *spiritual sight* became ever more clearly defined, the edifice of Anthroposophy—certainly incomplete in many ways.

But another requirement arose, different from that of elaborating Anthroposophy and devoting myself solely to problems connected with imparting facts directly from the spiritual world to the general cultural life of today: the requirement of meeting fully the inner need and spiritual longing of the members.

Requests were especially strong to shed the light of Anthroposophy upon the Gospels and the Bible in general. The members wished to have courses of lectures on these revelations bestowed upon humankind.

In meeting this need through private lecture courses, another factor arose: at these lectures only members were present. They were familiar with basic content of Anthroposophy. I could address them as people advanced in anthroposophical knowledge. The approach I adopted in these lectures was not at all suitable for the written works intended primarily for the general public.

In these private circles I could formulate what I had to say in a way I should have been *obliged* to modify had it been planned initially for the general public.

Thus the public and the private publications are in fact two quite different things, built upon different foundations. The public writings are the direct result of my inner struggles and labors, whereas the privately printed material includes the inner struggle and labor of the members. I listened to the inner needs of the members, and my living experience of this determined the form of the lectures.

However, nothing was ever said that was not solely the result of my direct experience of the growing content of Anthroposophy. There was never any question of concessions to the prejudices or the preferences of the members. Whoever reads these privately printed lectures can take them to represent Anthroposophy in the fullest sense. Thus it was possible without hesitation—when the complaints in this direction became too persistent—to depart from the custom of circulating this material only among members. But it must be borne in mind that faulty passages occur in these lecture-reports not revised by myself.

The right to judge such private material can, of course, be conceded only to someone who has the prerequisite basis for such judgment. And in respect of most of this material it would mean *at least* knowledge of the human being and of the cosmos insofar as these have been presented in the light of Anthroposophy, and also knowledge of what exists as "anthroposophical history" in what has been imparted from the spiritual world.

Extract from *Rudolf Steiner, An Autobiography,*
2nd ed. (New York: Steinerbooks, 1980), 386–88.

SYNOPSIS OF THE LECTURES

LECTURE 1

The need for a new art of education. The *whole* of life must be considered. Process of incarnation as a stupendous task of the spirit. Fundamental changes at seven and fourteen. At seven, the forming of the "new body" out of the "model body" inherited at birth. After birth, the bodily milk as sole nourishment. The teacher's task to give "soul milk" at the change of teeth and "spiritual milk" at puberty.

LECTURE 2

In first epoch of life child is wholly sense organ. Nature of child's environment and conduct of surrounding adults of paramount importance. Detailed observation of children and its significance. In second epoch, seven to fourteen, fantasy and imagination as life blood of all education, e.g., in teaching of writing and reading, based on free creative activity of each teacher. The child as integral part of the environment until nine. Teaching about nature must be based on this. The "higher truths" in fairy tales and myths. How the teacher can guide the child through the critical moment of the ninth year.

LECTURE 3

How to teach about plants and animals (seven to fourteen). Plants must always be considered, not as specimens, but growing in the soil. The plant belongs to the *earth*. This is the true picture and gives the child an inward joy. Animals must be spoken of always in connection with *humans*. All animal qualities and physical characteristics are to be found, in some form, in the human being. Humans as synthesis of the whole animal kingdom. Minerals should not be introduced until twelfth year. History should first be presented in living, imaginative pictures, through legends, myths, and stories. Only at eleven or twelve should any teaching be based on cause and effect, which is foreign to the young child's nature. Some thoughts on punishment, with examples.

taught, out of feeling, eurythmy will develop naturally, expressing inner and outer experiences in ordered movements—"visible speech." Finding relationship to space in *gymnastics*.

LECTURE 7
Between seven and fourteen *soul* qualities are paramount. Beginnings of *science teaching* from twelfth year only, and connected with real phenomena of life. The problem of *fatigue*. Wrong conceptions of psychologists. The rhythmic system, predominant in second period, never tires. Rhythm and fantasy. *Composition*. *Sums* from real life, not abstractions. Einstein's theory. The *kindergarten*—imitation of life. *Teachers' meetings*, the heart of the school. Every child to be in the right class for its age. Importance of some knowledge of trades, e.g., shoemaking, *handwork*, and embroidery. *Children's reports*—characterization, but no grading. Contact with the *parents*.

QUESTIONS AND ANSWERS
The close relationship of *Multiplication and Division*. How to deal with both together. *Transition from the concrete to the abstract in Arithmetic*. Not before the ninth year. Healthiness of English weights and measures as related to real life. Decimal system as an intellectual abstraction.

Drawing. Lines have no reality in drawing and painting, only *boundaries*. How to teach children to draw a tree in shading, speaking only of light and color. (Illustration). Line drawing belongs only to geometry.

Gymnastics and Sport. Sport is of no *educational* value, but necessary as belonging to English life. Gymnastics should be taught by demonstration.

Religious Instruction. Religion lessons in the Waldorf school given by Catholic priest and Protestant pastor. "Free" religion lessons provided for the other children. Plan of such teaching described, of which the fundamental aim is an understanding of Christianity. The Sunday services.

Modern Language Lessons. Choice of languages must be guided by the demands of English life. These can be introduced at an early age. Direct method in language teaching.

Closing words by Dr. Steiner on the seriousness of this first attempt to found a school in England.

INTRODUCTION

by Christopher Bamford

Introduction

These talks, translated as *The Kingdom of Childhood*, were given by Rudolf Steiner at the Second International Summer Conference, arranged by D. N. Dunlop and E. C. Merry, in Torquay, England, in August, 1924. [1] Rudolf Steiner was then already a sick man. It was his last trip after a quarter of a century of tirelessly crisscrossing the length and breadth of Europe in the service of renewed spiritual knowledge. Günther Wachsmuth, who was one of those who travelled with him, writes:

During the summer conference in Torquay, [Rudolf Steiner] suffered tragically from the destructive illness. Outwardly, however, nothing of this could be seen. Every day he met all the requirements of the comprehensive program and his lecturing activity. He spoke introductory words at artistic programs, held numerous conferences, took part in excursions. But every meal caused renewed suffering in his illness, a condition which he bore courageously, without a word of complaint. Dr. Wegman, his faithful physician, discussed the situation with me and found inconspicuous ways of enabling him to reduce his suffering during trips, and during pauses in the program, and at mealtimes. But Rudolf Steiner allowed nothing of

1. See T. H. Meyer, *D. N. Dunlop, A Man of Our Time*. London: Temple Lodge, 1992; also Günther Wachsmuth, *The Life and Work of Rudolf Steiner.* Blauvelt, New York: Spiritual Science Library, 1989.

this illness to be known by those at the conference. The more his physical suffering increased, the more heroic became his concentrated, intense, and at the same time spiritually clarified activity to bring about and safeguard the greatest plenitude of spiritual knowledge in this life on earth.[2]

The theme of Steiner's main lectures was *Initiation Consciousness: True and False paths in Spiritual Investigation*.[3] From August 11 to 22, this cycle was given in the mornings in the Town Hall. In the afternoons, a small group of aspirant teachers, who hoped to open a Waldorf School in England, met for an impromptu education course. But this was by no means the end of Rudolf Steiner's activities. In the evenings, there were special lectures on, among other topics, the Christmas Conference, the workings of destiny, Christendom and the impulse of Arabism, and the Anthroposophical Movement and the Grail and Arthur streams. There were also eurythmy performances and evenings of music and poetry. One evening, Rudolf Steiner held a lecture for the First Class of the School of Spiritual Science. And, on August 17, there was a fifty mile journey, across the moors of Dartmoor, to Tintagel where King Arthur's castle had once stood.[4]

Such then was the immediate context of the lectures on education printed here. This was by no means the first time that Steiner had spoken on Waldorf education in England, nor were the ideas new on English soil. Already in 1919 a group had come together in Kings Langley to seek to find a way of realizing Steiner's educational ideals. Among these was H. Millicent

2. Wachsmuth, op. cit.
3. Rudolf Steiner, *True and False Paths in Spiritual Investigation*. London: Rudolf Steiner Press, 1985.
4. See Meyer op. cit., Dunlop op. cit., and Rudolf Steiner, *The Archangel Michael*, pp. 269–282. Hudson, New York: Anthroposophic Press, 1994.

MacKenzie, Professor of Education at the University College Cardiff, who went to Berlin where she met Rudolf Steiner.[5] As a result of this meeting, and following her attendance at the Christmas Course for teachers at the Goetheanum in 1921, Rudolf Steiner was invited to speak during the Shakespeare Festival at Stratford on Avon on "New Ideals in Education."[6] The *London Times* reported:

The famous person in this years conference was Dr. Rudolf Steiner, who is distinguished at present not only in the field of education but also in other fields. In the light of spiritual science, he gives new forces of life to a number of dogmas hitherto held in check, and he promises to teacher relief from unnecessary difficulty through learning to know the soul of the child with the help of supersensible knowledge. [7]

During this trip, Steiner spent time in Kings Langley discussing educational matters with Miss Cross of the Priory School.

In August of the following year (1922), Steiner returned to England to attend the "Oxford Holiday Conference" at Mansfield College on "Spiritual Values in Education and Social Life." This was organized by Millicent Mackenzie, who took the chair, and opened by L. P. Jacks, Principle of Manchester College. As the *Oxford Chronicle* reported:

Approximately 200 students are taking part in this Congress. Presiding at the conference is the Minister for Labor,

5. H. Millicent MacKenzie was a well-known educator. She was the author of *Freedom in Education. An Inquiry into its Meaning, Value, and Condition.* London: Hodder and Staughton, 1925. She also wrote *Hegel's Theory and Practice of Education* (publisher and date unknown).
6. See Rudolf Steiner, *Waldorf Education and Anthroposophy I.* Hudson, New York: Anthroposophic Press, 1995.
7. Quoted Wachsmuth.

Dr. H. A. L. Fisher and prominent representatives of the most varied special fields are included in its council. Among the names of the lecturers are to be found those of Mr. Clutton Brock, Dr. Maxwell Garnett, Professor Gilbert Murray, Mr. Edmund Holmes, and others. The program thus comprises an extensive area of pedagogical ideals and endeavors.

The most prominent personality at the Congress is probably Dr. Rudolf Steiner.... Dr. Steiner speaks every forenoon on *The Spiritual Foundations of Education.*[8]

The following year, 1923, Rudolf Steiner again returned to England and carried the pedagogical work further. He gave a lecture on "Contemporary Spiritual Life and Education" under the auspices of the Union for the Realization of Spiritual Values in Education.[9] Then, before going on to the First International Summer School at Penmaemawr, he gave, among other lectures, the lecture course published under the title of *A Modern Art of Education.*[10] During this meeting, four women came to Steiner to ask him for advice on founding a school. He encouraged them to proceed with their plans, but advised them to plan a large school—for a small school would be a disadvantage in England. It should be modern and well thought out, and conversant with other contemporary educational ideas. For they were not to be dilettantish. This school, he advised, should be neither be in the country, nor in a poor neighborhood, like the East End of London. Nevertheless, it should be a

8. See Wachsmuth. Also Rudolf Steiner, *The Spiritual Ground of Education.* London: Anthroposophical Publishing Company, 1948.
9. See Rudolf Steiner, *Waldorf Education and Anthroposophy II.* Hudson, New York: Anthroposophic Press, 1995.
10. Rudolf Steiner, *A Modern Art of Education.* London: Rudolf Steiner Press, 1972; also available as *Education and Modern Spiritual Life.* Blauvelt, New York: Steinerbooks, 1989.

school for all children. In conclusion, he said, they must find a
man to work with them. This man turned out to be A. C. Harwood, who attended *The Kingdom of Childhood* lectures the
following year in Torquay. He had come there thinking it a
fine place to recuperate from a bout of mumps.

In his Preface to the previous edition of *The Kingdom of
Childhood*, this same A. C. Harwood wrote:

[These talks] were given specifically for a small group of
teachers or intending teachers, no more than five in number (though some others were allowed to attend), who had
resolved to open a school based on [Steiner's] work.[11]

As always, Rudolf Steiner adapted what he had to say to the
character of his special audience, some of whom had no experience of teaching. He gives them every possible encouragement,
while he points out the magnitude of the task on which they are
entering. He stimulates their observation by many practical and
homely examples. he shows them how essential it is for teachers
to work upon themselves, not merely to use their natural gifts
but to transform them, to seek for unsuspected powers within
themselves, never to become pedants, but to make ample use of
humor and keep their teaching and themselves lively and imaginative. But, above all, he insists on the grave importance of
doing everything in the light of the knowledge of the child as a
citizen of the spiritual as well as of the earthly world.

Many of the ideas which Steiner stressed forty years ago have
since appeared—in modified forms—in the general practice of
education. But there is no other form of education which
affirms the existence of the eternal being of the child in the
spiritual world before birth, which regards childhood as a gradual process of incarnation, and sees all physical processes as the

---

11. This was opened 1925 in 1925 as the New School in Streatham. It is now
known as Michael Hall and is situated in Forest Row. Sussex.

result of spiritual powers. This is the unique core of an anthroposophical education, and Steiner reminds teachers that they must never forget it or represent the methods developed in his schools apart from these central truths.

The reader of these lectures must bear in mind that, in giving them, Steiner assumed in his hearers some fundamental knowledge of that Spiritual Science which it had been his life's work to establish. Some of his statements may therefore appear to have a somewhat dogmatic flavor to a new reader who does not know what careful research and depth of study lie behind them.

In general, however, the lectures are concerned with practical examples, which give a lively picture of the kind of teaching Steiner wished to prevail in his schools. He himself described these lectures as "aphoristic," and sometimes they seem to treat in quick succession an almost bewildering number of subjects. But, on reflection, it will be found that they return again and again to a few central themes:

—the need for observation in the teacher;
—the dangers of stressing the intellect and handling the abstract before the age of adolescence;
—the crying in need in children for the concrete and pictorial;
—the education of the soul through wonder and reverence;
—the difference it makes to life when imagination first grasps the whole, and the part comes later in its proper relation; and, at the same time, the need for children to be practical and to understand the practical work of the world around them.

Steiner himself distinguished sharply between the styles appropriate to the written and the spoken word. Had he been able to revise these lectures as a book he would no doubt have transformed them radically. As this was not possible, it has seemed best to keep in the translation the colloquial style of the

original (and unrevised) typescript. The lectures should be read
as talks given to an intimate group.

The talks themselves are self-explanatory. As a lecture course,
they have always been in demand. Perhaps this is because they
were given originally to a small English group, dedicated to the
project of founding their own Waldorf School. And, for this
reason, perhaps, they have spoken directly and simply to all
those pioneer parents and teachers who over the past seventy or
so years have struggled to do the same in the English-speaking
world. They have always found these lectures especially excit-
ing and inspiring for their great *practical* value. And such practical value, after all, is at the heart of Waldorf education, as
Rudolf Steiner emphasizes in his seventh lecture:

If, therefore, we educate children not only out of
knowledge of the human being, but in accordance with
the demands of life, they will also have to know how to
read and write properly at the age when this is expected of
them today. We are obliged to include in the curriculum
many things that are simply demanded by the customs of
the time. Nevertheless, we must also try to bring the children into touch with life as much as possible.

I would dearly like to have a shoemaker in the Waldorf
School, if this were possible. It cannot be done because
such a thing does not fit into a curriculum based on
present-day requirements, but in order that the children
might really learn to make shoes, and to know, not theoretically but through their own work, what this entails, I
would dearly like to have a shoemaker on the staff of the
school. But it simply cannot be done because it is not in
accordance with the authorities, although it is just the very
thing that is in accordance with real life. Nevertheless, we
do try to enable the children to be practical workers.

1

My Dear Friends,

It gives me the deepest satisfaction to find here in England that you are ready to consider founding a school based on anthroposophical ideas.[1] This may be a truly momentous and incisive event in the history of education. Such words could well be heard as expressing lack of humility, but what will come about for education through an art of education based on Anthroposophy is something quite special. And I am overjoyed that an impulse has arisen to form the first beginnings of a College of Teachers, teachers who from the depths of their hearts do indeed recognize the very special quality of what we call anthroposophical education. It is no fanatical idea of reform that prompts us to speak of a renewal in educational life; we are urged to do so out of our whole feeling and experience of how humankind is evolving in civilization and in cultural life.

In speaking thus we are fully aware of the immense amount that has been done for education by distinguished individuals in the course of the nineteenth century, and especially in the last few decades. But although this was undertaken with the

---

1. "The New School," Streatham Hill, London, S.W.16, was opened in January 1925. In 1935 the name was changed to "Michael Hall." In 1945 the school was moved to Kidbrooke Park, Forest Row, Sussex.

very best intentions and every possible method was tried, a real knowledge of the human being has been lacking. These ideas about education arose at a time when no real knowledge of the human being was possible because of the materialism that prevailed in all aspects of life and indeed had done so since the fifteenth century. Therefore, when people expounded their ideas on educational reform they were building on sand or on something even less stable; rules of education were laid down based on all sorts of emotions and opinions of what life ought to be. It was impossible to know the wholeness of the human being and to ask the question: How can we bring to light in people what lies, god-given, within their nature after they have descended from pre-earthly life into earthly life? This is the kind of question that can be raised in an abstract way, but can only be answered concretely on the basis of a true knowledge of the human being in body, soul, and spirit.

Now this is how the matter stands for present-day humanity. The knowledge of the body is highly developed. By means of biology, physiology, and anatomy a very advanced knowledge of the human body has been acquired; but as soon as we wish to acquire a knowledge of the soul, we, with our present-day views, are confronted with a complete impasse, for everything relating to the soul is merely a name, a word. Even for such things as thinking, feeling, and willing we find no reality in the ordinary psychology of today. We still use the words thinking, feeling, and willing, but there is no conception of what takes place in the soul in reference to these things. What the so-called psychologists have to say about thinking, feeling, and willing is in reality mere dilettantism. It is just as though a physiologist were to speak in a general way of the human lungs or liver, making no distinction between the liver of a child and that of an old person. We are advanced in the science of the body; no physiologist would fail to note the difference between the lungs of a child and the lungs of an old man, or indeed, between the hair of a child and the hair of an old man. A physiologist would note all these differences. But thinking, feeling, and willing are mere words that are uttered without conveying any sense of reality. For instance, it is not known that willing, as it appears in the soul, is young, while thinking is old; that in fact thinking is willing grown old, and willing is a youthful thinking in the soul. Thus everything that pertains to the soul contains youthfulness and old age, both existing in human beings simultaneously.

Even in the soul of a young child there is the old thinking and the young willing together at the same time. Indeed, these things are realities. But today no one knows how to speak of these realities of the soul in the same way the realities of the body are spoken of, so that as teachers of children we are quite helpless. Suppose you were a physician and yet were unable to distinguish between a child and an old man! You would of course feel helpless. But since there is no science of the soul the teacher is unable to speak about the human soul as the modern physician can of the human body. And as for the spirit, there is no such thing! One cannot speak of it, there are no longer even any words for it. There is but the single word "spirit," and that does not convey much. There are no other words to describe it.

In our present-day life we cannot therefore venture to speak of a knowledge of the human being. Here we may easily feel that all is not well with our education, and that certain things must be improved upon. Yes, but how can we improve matters if we know nothing at all of the human being? Therefore all the ideas for improving education may be inspired by the best will in the world, but they possess no knowledge of the human being.

This can be noticed even in our own circles. For today it is Anthroposophy that can help us to acquire this knowledge of human beings. I am not saying this from any sectarian or fanatical standpoint, but it is true that one who seeks knowledge of the human being must find it in Anthroposophy. It is obvious that knowledge of the human being must be the basis for a teacher's work; that being so, teachers must acquire this knowledge for themselves, and the natural thing will be that they acquire it through Anthroposophy. If, therefore, we are asked what the basis of a new method of education should be, our answer is: Anthroposophy must be that basis. But how many people there are, even in our own circles, who try to disclaim Anthroposophy as much as possible, and to propagate an education without letting it be known that Anthroposophy is behind it.

An old German proverb says: Please wash me but don't make me wet! Many projects are undertaken in this spirit but you must above all both speak and think truthfully. So if anyone asks you how to become a good teacher you must say: Make Anthroposophy your foundation. You must not deny Anthroposophy, for only by this means can you acquire your knowledge of the human being.

There is no knowledge of the human being in our present cultural life. There are theories, but no living insights, either into the world, life, or people. A true insight will lead to a true practice in life, but there is no such practical life today. Do you know who are the most unpractical people at the present time? It is not the scientists, for although they are awkward and ignorant of life, these faults can be seen clearly in them. But these things are not observed in those who truly are the worst theorists and who are the least practical in life. They are the so-called practical people, the business and industry people and bankers, those who rule the practical affairs of life with theoretical thoughts. A bank today is entirely composed of thoughts arising from theories. There is nothing practical in it; but people do not notice this, for they say: It must be so, that is the way practical people work. So they adapt themselves to it, and no one notices the harm that is really being done in life because it is all worked in such an unpractical way. The "practical life" of today is absolutely unpractical in all its forms.

This will be noticed only when an ever-increasing number of destructive elements enter our civilization and break it up. If this goes on the World War will have been nothing but a first step, an introduction. In reality the World War arose out of this unpractical thinking, but that was only an introduction. The point now at stake is that people should not remain asleep any longer, particularly in teaching and education. Our task is to introduce an education that concerns itself with the whole person—body, soul, and spirit—and these three principles will become known and recognized.

In the short course that is to be given here I can speak only of the most important aspects of body, soul, and spirit, in such a way that it will give a direction to education and teaching. That is what I shall do. But the first requirement, as will be seen from the start, is that my listeners must really try to direct their observation, even externally, to the whole human being.

How are the basic principles of education determined these days? The child is observed, and then you are told, the child is like this or like that, and must learn something. Then it is thought how best to teach so that the child can learn such and such a thing quickly. But what, in reality, is a child? A child remains a child for at most twelve years, or possibly longer, but that is not the point. The point is that a child must always be thought of as becoming a grown-up person someday. Life as a whole is a unity, and you must not consider only the child but the whole of life; you must look at the whole human being.

Suppose I have a pale child in the school. A pale child should be an enigma to me, a riddle to be solved. There may be several reasons for the pallor, but the following is a possible one. The child may have come to school with somewhat rosy cheeks, and my treatment of the child may have caused the pallor. I must admit this and be able to judge the causes of the change of color; I may perhaps come to see that I have given this child too much to learn by heart. The memory may have been worked too hard. If I do not admit this possibility, if I am a shortsighted teacher with the idea that a method must be carried through regardless of whether the child grows rosy or pale thereby, that the method must be preserved at any cost, then the child will remain pale.

If, however, I observed this same child at the age of fifty, I would probably find terrible sclerosis or arterial hardening, the cause of which would be unknown. This is the result of my having overloaded the child's memory at the age of eight or nine. For you see, the adult of fifty and the child of eight or nine belong together, they are one and the same human being. I must know what the result will be, forty or fifty years later, of my management of the child; for life is a unity, it is all connected. It is not enough merely to know the child, I must know the whole human being.

Again, I take great trouble to give a class the best definitions I can, so that the concepts can be firmly grasped and the children will know: this is a lion, that is a cat, and so on. But should children retain these concepts to the day of their death? In our present age there is no feeling for the fact that the soul too must grow! If I furnish a child with a concept that is to remain "correct" (and "correctness" is of course all that matters!), a concept to be retained throughout life, it is just as though I bought the child a pair of shoes at the age of three, and each successive year had shoes made of the same size. The child will grow out of them. This however is something that people notice, and it would be considered brutal to try and keep the child's feet small enough to go on wearing the same sized shoes! Yet this is what is being done with the soul when I furnish the child with ideas that do not grow with the person. I am constantly squeezing the soul into the ideas I give the child when I give concepts that are intended to be permanent; when I worry the child with fixed, unchangeable concepts, instead of giving the child concepts capable of expansion.

These are some of the ways in which you may begin to answer the challenge that in education you must take the whole human being into consideration—the growing, living human being, and not just an abstract idea.

It is only when you have the right conception of human life as a connected whole that you come to realize how different from each other the various ages are. Children before the first teeth are shed are very different beings from what they become afterwards. Of course, you must not interpret this in crudely formed judgments, but if you are capable of making finer distinctions in life, you can observe that children are quite different before and after the change of teeth.

Before the change of teeth you can still see quite clearly at work the effects of the child's habits of life before birth or conception, in its pre-earthly existence in the spiritual world. The body of the child acts almost as though it were spirit, for the spirit that has descended from the spiritual world is still fully active in a child in the first seven years of life. You will say: A fine sort of spirit! It has become quite boisterous; for the child is rampageous, awkward, and incompetent. Is all this to be attributed to the spirit belonging to its pre-earthly life? Well, my dear friends, suppose all you clever and well-brought-up people were suddenly condemned to remain always in a room having a temperature of 144° Fahrenheit? You couldn't do it! It is even harder for the spirit of the child, which has descended from the spiritual worlds, to accustom itself to earthly conditions. The spirit, suddenly transported into a completely different world, with the new experience of having a body to carry about, acts as we see the child act. Yet if you know how to observe and note how each day, each week, each month, the indefinite features of the face become more definite, the awkward movements become less clumsy, and the child gradually accustoms itself to its surroundings, then you will realize that it is the spirit from the pre-earthly world that is working to make the child's body gradually more like itself. We shall understand why the child is as it is if we observe the child in this way, and we shall also understand it is the descended spirit that is acting as we see it within the child's body. Therefore for someone who knows the mysteries of the spirit it is both wonderful and delightful to observe a little child. In doing so one learns not of the earth, but of heaven.

In so-called "good children," as a rule, their bodies have already become heavy, even in infancy, and the spirit cannot properly take hold of the body. Such children are quiet; they do not scream and rush about, they sit still and make no noise. The spirit is not active within them, because their bodies offer such resistance. It is often the case that the bodies of so-called good children offer resistance to the spirit.

In the less well-behaved children who make a great deal of healthy noise, who shout properly, and give a lot of trouble, the spirit is active, though of course in a clumsy way, for it has been transported from heaven to earth; but the spirit is active within them. It is making use of the body. You may even regard the wild screams of a child as most enthralling, simply because you thereby experience the martyrdom the spirit has to endure when it descends into a child-body.

Yes, my dear friends, it is easy to be a grown-up person—easy for the spirit, I mean, because the body has then been made ready, it no longer offers the same resistance. It is quite easy to be a full-grown person but extremely difficult to be a child. The child itself is not aware of this because consciousness is not yet awake. It is still asleep, but if the child possessed the consciousness it had before descending to earth it would soon notice this difficulty: if the child were still living in this pre-earthly consciousness its life would be a terrible tragedy, a really terrible tragedy. For you see, the child comes down to earth; before this it has been accustomed to a spiritual substance from which it drew its spiritual life. The child was accustomed to deal with that spiritual substance. It had prepared itself according to its karma, according to the result of previous lives. It was fully contained within its own spiritual garment, as it were. Now it has to descend to earth. I should like to speak quite simply about these things, and you must excuse me if I speak of them as I would if I were describing the ordinary things of the earth. I can speak of them thus because they are so. Now when a human being is to descend, a body must be chosen on the earth.

And indeed this body has been prepared throughout generations. Some father and mother had a son or a daughter, and there again a son or a daughter, and so on. Thus through heredity a body is produced that must now be occupied. The spirit must draw into it and dwell in it; but in so doing it is suddenly faced with quite different conditions. It clothes itself in a body that has been prepared by a number of generations.

Of course, even from the spiritual world the human being can work on the body so that it may not be altogether unsuitable, yet as a rule the body received is not so very suitable after all. For the most part a soul does not fit at all easily into such a body. If a glove were to fit your hand as badly as the body generally fits the soul, you would discard it at once. You would never think of putting it on. But when you come down from the spiritual world needing a body, you just have to take one; and you keep this body until the change of teeth. For it is a fact that every seven or eight years our external physical substance is completely changed, at least in the essentials, though not in all respects. Our first teeth for instance are changed, the second set remain. This is not the case with all the members of the human organism; some parts, even more important than the teeth, undergo change every seven years as long as a person is on the earth. If the teeth were to behave in the same way as these we should have new teeth at seven, fourteen, and again at twenty-one years of age, and so on—and there would be no dentists in the world.

Thus certain hard organs remain, but the softer ones are constantly being renewed. In the first seven years of our life we have a body that is given to us by outer nature, by our parents, and so on; it is a model. The soul occupies the same relation to this body as an artist to a model that he has to copy. We gradually shape the second body out of the first body up to the change of teeth. It takes seven years to complete the process. This second body that we ourselves have fashioned on the model given us by our parents only appears at the end of the first seven years of life, and all that external science says today about heredity and so forth is mere dilettantism compared to the reality. In reality we receive at birth a model body that is with us for seven years, although during the very first years of life it begins to die out and fall away. The process continues, until at the change of teeth we have our second body.

Now there are weak individualities who are weakly when they descend to earth; these form their second body, in which they will live after the change of teeth, as an exact copy of the first one. People say that they take after their parents by inheritance, but this is not true. They make their own second body according to the inherited model. It is only during our first seven years of life that the body is really inherited, but naturally many are weak individualities and copy a great deal. There are also strong individualities descending to earth, and they too inherit a good deal in the first seven years, which can be observed in their teeth. The first teeth are still soft and subject to heredity, but when they are strong individualities, developing in the proper way, these children will have good strong second teeth. There are children who at ten years of age are just like children of four—mere imitators. Others are quite different, strong individuality stirs within them. The model is used, but afterward they form an individual body for themselves.

Such things must be noted. All talk of heredity will not lead you far unless you realize how matters stand. Heredity, in the sense that it is spoken of by science, only applies to the first seven years of a person's life. After that age, whatever we inherit is inherited of our own free will, we might say; we imitate the model, but in reality the inherited part is thrown off with the first body at the change of teeth.

The soul nature that comes down from the spiritual world is very strong in us, and it is clumsy at first because it has to become accustomed to external nature. Yet in reality everything about a child, even the worst naughtiness, is very fascinating. Of course we must follow the conventions to some extent and not allow all naughtiness to pass unreproved; but we can see better in children than anywhere else how the spirit of the human being is tormented by the demons of degeneracy that are present in the world. The child has to enter a world into which it so often does not fit. If you were conscious of this process, you would see how terribly tragic it is. When you know something of initiation, and are able to consciously observe what lays hold of the child's body, it really is terrible to see how the child must find a way into all the complications of bones and ligaments that have to be formed. It really is a tragic sight.

The child knows nothing of this, for the Guardian of the Threshold protects the child from any such knowledge. But teachers should be aware of it and look on with the deepest reverence, knowing that here a being whose nature is of God and the spirit has descended to earth. The essential thing is that you should know this, that you should fill your hearts with this knowledge, and from this starting point undertake your work as educators.

There are great differences between the manner of human being that a person is in the spiritual-soul life before descending to earth, and that which a person has to become here below. Teachers should be able to judge this because standing before them is the child in whom are the aftereffects of the spiritual world. Now there is one thing that the child has difficulty in acquiring, because the soul had nothing of this in the spiritual life.

On earth, human beings have little ability to direct their attention to the inner part of the body; that is only done by the natural scientists and the physicians. They know exactly what goes on inside a person within the limits of the skin, but you will find that most people do not even know exactly where their heart is! They generally point to the wrong place, and if in the course of social life today a person was asked to explain the difference between the lobes of the right and left lungs, or to describe the duodenum, very curious answers would be given. Now before we come down into earthly life we take little interest in the external world, but we take much more interest in what may be called our spiritual inner being. In the life between death and a new birth our interest is almost entirely centered on our inner spiritual life. We build up our karma in accordance with experiences from previous earth lives and this we develop according to our inner life of spirit. The interest that we take in it is far removed from any earthly quality, very far removed from that longing for knowledge that, in its one-sided form, may be called inquisitiveness. A longing for knowledge, curiosity, a passionate desire for knowledge of the external life was not ours before our birth or descent to earth; we did not know it at all. That is why the young child has it only in so slight a degree.

What we do experience, on the other hand, is to live right in and with our environment. Before descending to earth we live entirely in the outer world. The whole world is then our inner being and there exist no such distinctions as outer and inner world. Therefore we are not curious about what is external, for that is all within us. We have no curiosity about it, we bear it within us, and it is an obvious and natural thing that we experience.

So in the first seven years of life a child learns to walk, to speak, and to think, out of the same manner of living it had before descending to earth. If you try to arouse curiosity in a child about some particular word, you will find that you thereby entirely drive out the child's wish to learn that word. If you count on a longing for knowledge or curiosity you drive out just what the child ought to have. You must not reckon on a child's curiosity, but rather on something else, namely, that the child becomes merged into you as it were, and you really live in the child. All that the child enjoys must live and be as though it were the child's own inner nature. You must make the same impression on the child as its own arm makes. You must, so to say, be only the continuation of its own body. Then later, when the child has passed through the change of teeth and gradually enters the period between seven and fourteen years old, you must observe how, little by little, curiosity and a longing for knowledge begin to show themselves; you must be tactful and careful, and pay attention to the way in which curiosity gradually stirs into being within the child.

The small child is still only a clumsy little creature, who does not ask questions, and you can only make an impression by being something yourself. A child questions the environment as little as a sack of flour. But just as a sack of flour will retain any impressions you make upon it (especially if it is well ground), so too does the little child retain impressions, not because the child is curious, but because you yourself are really one with the child and make impressions as you would do with your fingers on a sack of flour.

It is only at the change of teeth that the situation alters. You must notice the way the child now begins to ask questions. "What is that? What do the stars see with? Why are the stars in the sky? Why have you a crooked nose, grandmother?" The child now asks all kinds of questions and begins to be curious about surrounding things. You must have a delicate perception and note the gradual beginnings of curiosity and attention that appear with the second teeth. These are the years when these qualities appear and you must be ready to meet them. You must allow the child's inner nature to decide what you ought to be doing; I mean, you must take the keenest interest in what is awakening with the change of teeth.

A very great deal is awakening then. The child is curious, but not with an intellectual curiosity, for as yet the child has no reasoning powers; and anyone who tries to appeal to the intellect of a child of seven is quite on the wrong lines. The child has fantasy, and this fantasy is what we must engage. It is really a question of developing the concept of a kind of "milk of the soul." For you see, after birth the child must be given bodily milk. This constitutes its food and every other necessary substance is contained in the milk that the child consumes. And when children come to school at the age of the changing of the teeth it is again milk that you must give them, but now, milk for the soul. That is to say, your teaching must not be made up of isolated units, but all that the children receive must be a unity; after the change of teeth children must have "soul milk." If they are taught to read and write as two separate things it is just as though their milk were to be separated chemically into two different parts, and you gave them one part at one time and the other at another. Reading and writing must form a unity. You must bring this idea of "soul milk" into being for your work with the children when they first come to school.

This can only come about if, after the change of teeth, the children's education is directed artistically. The artistic element must be in it all. Tomorrow I will describe more fully how to develop writing out of painting and thus give it an artistic form, and how you must then lead this over artistically to the teaching of reading, and how this artistic treatment of reading and writing must be connected, again by artistic means, with the first simple beginnings of arithmetic. All this must thus form a unity. You must gradually develop such things as "soul milk" for the children when they come to school.

And when children reach the age of puberty they will require "spiritual milk." This is extremely difficult to give to present-day humanity, for there is no spirit left in our materialistic age. It will be a difficult task to create "spiritual milk", but if you do not succeed in creating it yourselves, your boys and girls will be left to themselves during the difficult adolescent years, for there is otherwise no "spiritual milk" in our present age.

I just wanted to say these things by way of introduction and to give you a certain direction of thought; tomorrow we will continue these considerations and go more into details.

2

I pointed out yesterday how the child's development undergoes a radical change with the loss of the first teeth. For in truth, what we call heredity or inherited characteristics are only directly active during the first epoch of life. It is however the case that during the first seven years a second life organism is gradually built up in the physical body, which is fashioned after the model of the inherited organism. This second organism is completed at the changing of the teeth. If the individual who comes out of the spiritual pre-earthly world is weak, then this second life organism is similar to the inherited one. If the individual is strong, then we see how in the period between the change of teeth and puberty, from seven years till about fourteen, a kind of victory is gradually achieved over the inherited characteristics. Children become quite different, and they change even in their outward bodily form.

It is especially interesting to follow the qualities of soul that now reveal themselves in this second life epoch. In the first epoch, before the change of teeth, the child can be described as being wholly "sense-organ." You must take this quite literally: wholly sense-organ.

Take for example the human eye or ear. What is the characteristic of such a sense-organ? It is that the sense-organ is acutely sensitive to the impressions of the outer world. And if you observe the eye you can certainly see what kind of process takes place. The child during the first seven years is really completely and wholly an eye. Now consider only this thought: in the eye a picture is formed, an inverted picture, of every external object. This is what ordinary physics teaches everyone. What is outside in the world is to be found within the eye as a picture. Physics stops here, but this picture-forming process is really only the beginning of what you should know concerning the eye; it is the most external physical fact.

If physicists looked at this picture with a finer sense of observation, they would see that it determines the course of the circulation of the blood in the choroid. The whole choroid is conditioned in its blood circulation by the nature of this picture within the eye. The whole eye adjusts itself according to these things. These finer processes are not taken into consideration by ordinary physics. But the child during the first seven years is really an eye. If something takes place in the child's environment, let us say, to take an example, a fit of temper when someone becomes furiously angry, then the whole child will have an internalized picture of this outburst of rage. The etheric body makes a picture of it. From it something passes over into the entire circulation of the blood and the metabolic system, something that is related to this outburst of anger.

This is so in the first seven years, and the organism adjusts itself accordingly. Naturally these are not crude happenings, they are delicate processes. But if a child grows up with an angry father or a hot-tempered teacher, then the vascular system, the blood vessels, will follow the line of the anger. The results of this implanted tendency in the early years will then remain through the whole rest of life.

These are the things that matter most for young children. What you say, what you teach, does not yet make an impression, except insofar as children imitate what you say in their own speech. But it is what you *are* that matters; if you are good this goodness will appear in your gestures; and if you are bad-tempered this also will appear in your gestures—in short, everything that you do yourself passes over into the children and makes its way within them. This is the essential point. Children are wholly sense-organ, and react to all the impressions of the people around them. Therefore the essential thing is not to imagine that children can learn what is good or bad, that they can learn this or that, but to know that everything that is done in their presence is transformed in their childish organisms into spirit, soul, and body. The health of children for their whole life depends on how you conduct yourself in their presence. The inclinations that children develop depends on how you behave in their presence.

But all the things that you are usually advised to do with kindergarten children are quite worthless. The things that are introduced as kindergarten education are usually extraordinarily "clever." You could be quite fascinated by the cleverness of what has been thought out for kindergartens in the course of the nineteenth century. The children certainly learn a great deal there, they almost learn to read. They are supplied with letters of the alphabet which they have to fit into cut out letters. It all looks very clever and you can easily be tempted to believe that it really is something suitable for children, but it is of no use at all. It really has no value whatsoever, and the soul of the child is impaired by it. The child is damaged even down into the body, right down into physical health. Such kindergarten methods breed weaklings in body and soul for later life.[1]

---

1. *Translator's Note.* In Germany the children remain in the "kindergarten" until their seventh year so that the above remarks apply to all school life up to this time, (including, for instance, the "Infants" departments of state schools in England).

On the other hand, if you simply have the children there in the kindergarten and conduct yourselves so that they can imitate you, if you do all kinds of things that the children can copy out of their own inner impulse of soul, as they had been accustomed to do in pre-earthly existence, then indeed the children will become like yourself, but it is for you to see that you are worthy of this imitation. This is what you must pay attention to during the first seven years of life and not what you express outwardly in words as a moral idea.

If you make a surly face so that a child gets the impression you are a grumpy person, this harms the child for the rest of its life. This is why it is so important, especially for little children, that as a teacher you should enter very thoroughly into the observation of a human being and human life. What kind of school plan you make is neither here nor there; what matters is what sort of a person you are. In our day it is easy enough to think out a curriculum, because everyone in our age is now so clever. I am not saying this ironically; in our day people really are clever. Whenever a few people get together and decide that this or that must be done in education, something clever always comes out of it. I have never known a stupid educational program; they are always very clever. But what is important is that you have people in the school who can work in the way I have indicated. You must develop this way of thinking, for an immense amount depends upon it, especially for that age or life epoch of children in which they are really entirely sense-organ.

After the change of teeth is completed, children are no longer a sense-organ to the same degree as before. This is already diminishing between the third and fourth year. But before then children have quite special peculiarities that are generally not known whatsoever. When you eat something sweet or sour you perceive it on the tongue and palate, but when young children drink milk they feel that taste of milk through their whole body because they are also an organ of sense regarding taste. Young children taste with their whole body; there are many remarkable instances of this.

Older children take their cue from grown-ups and therefore at fifteen, sixteen, or twenty they are, nowadays, already blasé and have lost their freshness. But it is possible to find children in their earlier years who are still wholly sense-organ, though life is not easy for such. I knew for example a small boy who on being given something to eat that he knew he would enjoy, approached the delectable object not only with those organs with which a person generally approaches food, but he steered toward it with his hands and feet; he was in fact wholly an organ of taste. The remarkable thing is that in his ninth or tenth year he became a splendid eurythmist and developed a great understanding for eurythmy. So what he began by "padding" up to his food as a little child was developed further in his will organs at a later age.

I do not say these things jokingly, but to give you examples of how to observe. You very rarely hear people relating such things, but they are happening every moment. People fail to perceive these characteristic phenomena of life and only think about how to educate the young instead of observing life itself. Life is interesting in every detail, from morning till evening; the smallest things are interesting. Notice, for instance, how two people take a pear from a fruit bowl. No two people take the pear in the same way; it is always different. The whole character of a person is expressed in the way the pear is taken from the fruit dish and put on the plate, or straight into the mouth as the case may be.

If people would only cultivate more power of observation of this kind, the distressing things would not develop in schools that are unfortunately so often seen today. One scarcely sees a child now who holds a pen or pencil correctly. Most children hold them incorrectly, and it is because the teachers do not know how to observe the children properly. This is a very difficult thing to do, and it is not easy in the Waldorf school either, where drastic changes are frequently needed in the way the children hold their pencils or pens. You must never forget that the human being is a whole, and as such must acquire dexterity in all directions. Therefore what teachers need is observation of life down to the minutest details.

And if you especially like having formulated axioms, then take this as the first principle of a real art of education: You must be able to observe life in all its manifestations.

You can never learn enough in this regard. Look at the children from behind, for instance. Some walk by planting the whole foot on the ground, others trip along on their toes, and there can be every kind of differentiation between these two extremes. Yes, indeed, to educate a child you must know quite precisely how the child walks. For children who tread on their heels show in this small physical characteristic that they were very firmly planted in life in their former incarnation and were interested in everything in their former earth life. In such a case, you must draw as much as possible out of the child, for there are many things hidden away in children who walk strongly on their heels. On the other hand, the children who trip along, who scarcely use their heels in walking, have gone through their former earth life in a superficial way. You will not be able to get much out of these children, but when you are with them you must make a point of doing a great many things yourself that they can copy.

You should experience the changing of the teeth through careful observation like this. The fact that children were previously wholly sense-organ now enables them to develop above all the gift of fantasy and symbolism. And you must take this into consideration even in play. Our materialistic age sins terribly against this. Take for example the so-called beautiful dolls that are so often given to children these days. They have such beautifully formed faces, wonderfully painted cheeks, and even eyes with which they can go to sleep when laid down, real hair, and goodness knows what all! But this kills the fantasy of the child, for it leaves nothing to the imagination and the child can take no great pleasure in it. But if you make a doll out of a napkin or a handkerchief with two ink spots for eyes, a dab of ink for a mouth, and some sort of arms, then with imagination the child can add a great deal to it.

It is particularly good for children to be given the opportunity to add as much as possible to playthings out of their own fantasy. This enables children to develop a symbolizing activity. Children should have as few things as possible that are finished and complete and what people call "beautiful." For the beauty of such a doll that I have described above with real hair and so on, is only a conventional beauty. In truth it is ugly because it is so inartistic.

Do not forget that around the change of teeth children pass over into the period of imagination and fantasy. It is not the intellect but fantasy that fills life at this age. You as teachers must also be able to develop this life of fantasy, and those who bear a true knowledge of the human being in their souls are able to do this. It is indeed so that a true knowledge of the human being loosens and releases the inner life of soul and brings a smile to the face. Sour and grumpy faces come only from lack of knowledge. Certainly, a person can have a diseased organ that leaves traces of illness on the face; this does not matter, for the child is not affected by it. When the inner nature of a person is filled with a living knowledge of what the human being is, this will be expressed in his face, and this is what can make a really good teacher.

And so between the change of teeth and puberty you must educate out of the very essence of imagination. For the quality that makes a child under seven so wholly into a sense-organ now becomes more inward; it enters the soul life. The sense-organs do not think; they perceive pictures, or rather they form pictures from the external objects. And even when the child's sense experiences have already a quality of soul, it is not a thought that emerges but an image, albeit a soul image, an imaginative picture. Therefore in your teaching you must work in pictures, in images.

Now you can work least of all in pictures if you are teaching children something that is really quite foreign to them. For example, the calligraphy of today is quite foreign to children both in written or printed letters. They have no relation whatever to what is called an *A*. Why should they have a relation to an *A*? Why should they be interested in an *L*? These are quite foreign to them, this *A*, this *L*. Nevertheless when children come to school they are taught these things, with the result that they feel no contact with what they are doing. And if they are taught this before the change of teeth and are obliged to stick letters into cut-out holes, for example, then they are given things that are outside their nature and to which they have not the slightest relationship.

But what you should appeal to is what the children do possess now—an artistic sense, a faculty for creating imaginative pictures. It is to this you must turn. You should avoid a direct approach to the conventional letters of the alphabet that are used in writing and printing. Rather, you should lead the children, in a vivid and imaginative way, through the various stages that humanity has passed through in the history of civilization.

In former times there was picture writing; that is to say, people painted something on the page that reminded them of the object. You do not need to study the history of civilization, but you can show children the meaning and spirit of what people wanted to express in picture writing. Then children will feel at home in their lessons.

For example: Let us take the word *Mund*—(mouth). Get the children to draw a mouth, or rather paint it. Let them put on dabs of red color and then tell them to pronounce the word; you can say to them: don't pronounce the whole word at first, but begin only with the sound "M". And now you can form the *letter M* out of the upper lip (see drawing). If you follow this process you can get the letter *M* out of the mouth that the children first painted.

This is how writing really originated, even though today it is difficult to recognize from the words themselves that the letters were once pictures, because the words have all been subject to change in the course of the evolution of speech. Originally each sound had its own image and each picture could have but one meaning.

You do not need to go back to these original characters, but you can invent ways and means of your own. The teacher must be inventive and must create out of the spirit of the thing.

Take the word *fish*. Let the children draw or paint some kind of fish. Let them say the beginning of the word: "F" and you can gradually get the letter *F* out of the picture (see drawing).

And thus, if you are inventive, you can find pictures for all the consonants. They can be worked out from a kind of painting-drawing, or drawing-painting. This is more awkward to deal with than the methods of today. For it is of course necessary that after the children have been doing this painting for an hour or two you have to clear it all away. But it just has to be so, there is nothing else to be done.

So you can see how the letters can be developed out of pictures and the pictures again directly out of life. This is the way you must do it. On no account should you teach reading first, but proceeding from your drawing-painting and painting-drawing, you allow the letters to arise out of these, and then you can proceed to reading.

If you look around you will find plenty of objects that you can use to develop the consonants in this way. All the consonants can be developed from the initial letters of the words describing these objects.

It is not so easy for the vowels. But perhaps for the vowels the following is possible. Suppose you say to the children: "Look at the beautiful sun! You must really admire it; stand like this so that you can look up and admire the glorious sun." The children can stand, look up, and then express their wonder thus: Ah! Then you paint this gesture and you actually have the Hebrew *A*, the sound "Ah," the sound of wonder. Now you need only to make it smaller and gradually turn it into the letter *A* (see drawing).

And so if you bring before the children something of an inner soul quality and above all what is expressed in eurythmy, letting them take up one position or another, then you can also develop the vowels in the way I have mentioned.

Eurythmy will be a very great help to you because the sounds are already formed in the eurythmy gestures and movements. Think for instance of an *O*. You embrace something lovingly. Out of this you can obtain the *O* (see drawing). You can really get the vowels from the gesture, the movement.

( )

Thus you must work out of observation and imagination, and the children will then come to know the sounds and the letters from the things themselves. You must start from the picture. The letter, as we know it today in its finished form, has a history behind it. It is something that has been simplified from a picture, but the kind of magical signs of the printed letters of the present day no longer tell us what the pictures were like.

When the Europeans, these "better men," went to America at the time when the "savages," the native Indians, were still there—even in the middle of the nineteenth century such things happened—they showed these savages printed writing and the Indians ran away from it because they thought the letters were little devils. And they said: The palefaces, as the Indians called the Europeans, communicate with each other by means of little devils, little demons.

This is just what letters are for children. They mean nothing to them. The child feels something demonic in the letters, and rightly so. They already become a means of magic because they are merely signs.

You must begin with the picture. That is not a magic sign but something real and you must work from this.

People will object that the children then learn to read and write too late. This is said only because it is not known today how harmful it is when the children learn to read and write too soon. It is a very bad thing to be able to write early. Reading and writing as we have them today are really not suited to the human being till a later age—the eleventh or twelfth year—and the more a child is blessed with not being able to read and write well before this age, the better it is for the later years of life. A child who cannot write properly at thirteen or fourteen (I can speak out of my own experience because I could not do it at that age) is not so hindered for later spiritual development as one who early, at seven or eight years, can already read and write perfectly. These are things that the teacher must notice.

Naturally you will not be able to proceed as you really should today because the children have to pass from your independent school into public life. But a great deal can be done nevertheless when you know these things. It is a question of knowledge. And your knowledge must show you, above all, that it is quite wrong to teach reading before writing. In writing, especially if it is developed from the painting-drawing, drawing-painting that I have spoken of, the whole human being is active—the fingers take part, the body is positioned, the whole person is engaged. In reading only the head is occupied and anything that only occupies a part of the organism and leaves the remaining parts impassive should be taught as late as possible. It is most important first to bring the whole being into movement, and later on the single parts.

Naturally, if you want to work in this way you cannot expect to be given instructions for every detail, but only an indication of the path to be followed. And so you can build on nothing else but absolute freedom in this method of education arising out of Anthroposophy, though this freedom must include the free creative fancy of the teacher and educator.

In the Waldorf School we have been blessed with what I might call a very questionable success. We began with one hundred and thirty to one hundred and forty pupils; but these pupils came from the industrial works of Emil Molt, so they were at that time to a certain extent "compulsory" children, though we had also some children from anthroposophical families.[2] In the short time of its existence the Waldorf School has grown so big that we have now more than eight hundred children and between forty and fifty teachers. This is a doubtful success because gradually it becomes impossible to keep a clear view of the whole. From the arrangements of the Waldorf School that I shall describe to you, you will soon see how difficult it is to survey the whole; though I shall later indicate certain ways of making this possible. We have had to form parallel classes; in the case of the fifth and sixth there are three parallel classes: A, B, and C. These classes are still overfull and have more children than the other classes in the school.

There is therefore a teacher in Class A, another in Class B. Just imagine how this would work out in a "proper" educational establishment of today. You come into Class 1 A, where you find a particular educational drill going on that is considered the best. Now you go into Class 1 B. It could equally well be called "A," only that different children are sitting there, for in both classes exactly the same thing goes on, because the "right method" is used. This is of course all most clearly thought out: what is intellectual has but one meaning and it cannot be otherwise.

With us in the Waldorf School you find no such thing. You go into the first Class A. There you see a teacher, man or woman, who is teaching writing. The teacher lets the children make all kinds of forms, let us say with string. They then go on to painting the forms and gradually letters arise. A second teacher likes to do it differently. If you go into Class B you find

---

2. In 1919 the first Rudolf Steiner school was founded by Emil Molt, director of the Waldorf Astoria cigarette factory, Stuttgart. The first pupils were all children of the factory workers.

that this teacher is letting the children "dance" the forms round the room, in order that they may experience the forms of the letters in their own bodies. Then this teacher carries over these forms also into the letters themselves. You would never find uniformity of teaching in Classes A, B, and C. The same things are taught but in completely different ways, for a free creative imagination pervades the class. There are no prescribed rules for teaching in the Waldorf School, but only one unifying spirit that permeates the whole. It is very important that you under-stand this. Teachers are autonomous. Within this one unifying spirit they can do entirely what they think is right for them-selves. You will say: Yes, but if everyone can do as they like, then the whole school will fall into a chaotic condition. For in Class 5A, there could be goodness knows what kind of hocus-pocus going on, and in 5B, you might find them playing chess. But that is exactly what does not happen in the Waldorf School, for though there is freedom everywhere the spirit that is appropri-ate to the age of the children is active in each class.

If you read the "Seminar Course," you will see that you have the greatest liberty, and yet the teaching in each class is what is right for that age.[3] The strange thing is that no teacher has ever opposed this. They all quite voluntarily accept this principle of a unifying spirit in the work. No one opposes it or wants to have any special arrangements made. On the contrary, the wish is often expressed by the teachers to have as many discussions as possible in their meetings about what should be done in the various classes.

Why does no teacher object to the curriculum? The school

---

3. Just before the opening of the Waldorf School, in 1919, Dr. Steiner gave three simultaneous courses of lectures to the teachers two of which have been published in English under the titles of *Study of Man* and *Practical Advice to Teachers*.

has been going for several years. Why do you think that all the teachers approve of the curriculum? They do not find it at all unreasonable. They find it excellent in its very freedom because it is based upon real true human knowledge.

And the freedom that must prevail in the school can be seen in just such things as creating teaching matter out of imagination. Indeed it does. All of our teachers have the feeling that it is not only a question of what they think about and discover out of their own imagination, but when I sit with our Waldorf teachers in their meetings, or when I go into the classes, I get more and more the impression that once the teachers are in their classrooms they actually forget that a plan of teaching has previously been drawn up. What I experience when I go into the classes is that in the moment of teaching each teacher feels that he or she is creating the plan of work.

Such is the result when real human knowledge lies at the basis of the work. I tell you these details even though you might think they were said out of vanity; indeed they are not said out of vanity but so you know how it is and then go and do likewise; this will show you how what grows out of a true knowledge of the human being can really enter into the child.

Our teaching and education is to be built, then, on imagination. You must be quite clear that before the ninth or tenth year the child does not know how to differentiate itself as an ego from its surroundings. Out of a certain instinct children have long been accustomed to speak of themselves as "I," but in truth they really feel themselves within the whole world. However, people have the most fantastic ideas about this. They say of primitive races that their feeling for the world is "animism," that is, they treat lifeless objects as though they were "ensouled." They say that to understand children you must imagine that they do the same as these primitive peoples, that a child knocks against a hard object to endow it with a quality of soul.

But this is not at all true. In reality, children do not "ensoul" the object, but they do not yet distinguish between the living and the lifeless. For children, everything is one, and they are also one with their surroundings. Not until the age of nine or ten do children really learn to distinguish themselves from their environment. This is something you must take into consideration in the strictest sense to give your teaching a proper basis.

Therefore it is important to speak of everything that is around the children—plants, animals, and even stones—in a way that all these things talk to each other, that they act among themselves like human beings, that they tell each other things, that they love and hate each other. You must learn to use anthropomorphism in the most inventive ways and speak of plants and animals as though they were human. You must not "ensoul" them out of a kind of theory but treat them simply in a way that children can understand before they are able to distinguish between the lifeless and the living. As yet the child has no reason to think that the stone has no soul, whereas the dog has a soul. The first noticeable difference is that the dog moves, but the child does not attribute this movement to the fact that the dog has a soul. Indeed, you can treat all things that feel and live as if they were people, thinking, feeling, and speaking to one another, as if they were people with sympathy and antipathy for each other. Therefore everything that you bring to a child of this age must be given in the form of fairy tales, legends, and stories in which everything is endowed with feeling. It must be kept in mind that nourishing the instinctive soul qualities of imagination in this way is the best foundation for the child's soul life.

If you fill a child with all kinds of intellectual teaching during this age (and this will be the case if you do not transform everything you teach into pictures) then later the child will suffer effects in the blood vessels and circulation. You must consider the child in body, soul, and spirit as an absolute unity. This must be said repeatedly.

For this task as a teacher you must have artistic feeling in your soul and an artistic disposition. It is not only what you think out or what you can convey in ideas that works from teacher to child, but, if I may express myself so, it is the imponderable quality in life. A great deal passes over from teacher to child unconsciously. The teacher must be aware of this, above all when telling fairy tales, stories, or legends full of feeling. It can often be noticed in our materialistic times how a teacher does not really believe what he or she is telling and looks on it as something childish. It is here that Anthroposophy can be the guide and leader of a true knowledge of the human being. We become aware through Anthroposophy that we can express a thing infinitely more fully and more richly if we clothe it in pictures than if we put it into abstract ideas. A child who is healthy naturally feels the need to express everything in pictures and also to receive everything in picture form.

In this way Goethe learned to play the piano as a boy. He was shown how he had to use the first finger, the second finger, and so on; but he did not like this method, and his dry pedantic teacher was repugnant to him. Father Goethe was an old philistine, one of the old pedants of Frankfurt, who naturally preferred to engage philistine teachers, because they were the good ones, as everyone knew. But this kind of teaching was repugnant to the boy Goethe; it was too abstract. So he invented for himself the "Deuterling" ("the little fellow who points"), not "index finger," that was too abstract, but "Deuterling."[4]

---

4. Translator's note: Compare the old country names for the fingers referred to by Walter de la Mare in *Come Hither*, e.g., Tom Thumbkin, Bess Bumpkin, Long Linkin, Bill Wilkin, and Little Dick.

Children want an image, and want to think of themselves as an image, too. It is just in these things that we see how the teacher needs to use imagination, to be artistic, for then the teacher will meet the children with a truly "living" quality of soul. And this living quality works upon the children in an imponderable way—imponderable in the best sense.

Through Anthroposophy you learn once more to believe in legends, fairy tales, and myths, for they express a higher truth in imaginative pictures. And your handling of these fairy tales, legends, and mythical stories will once more be filled with a quality of soul. Then when you speak to the child, your very words, permeated by your own belief in the tales, will carry truth with them. Whereas it is so often untruth that passes between teacher and child, truth will flow between you and the child. Untruth at once holds sway if the teacher says: children are stupid, I am clever, children believe in fairy tales so I have to tell fairy tales to them. It's the proper thing for them to hear. When a teacher speaks like this then an intellectual element immediately enters into the storytelling.

But children, especially at the age between the change of teeth and puberty, are most sensitive as to whether teachers are governed by imagination or intellect. The intellect has a destructive and crippling effect on children; imagination gives children life and impulse.

It is vital that you make these fundamental thoughts your own. I will speak of them in greater detail during the next few days, but there is one more thing I would like to put before you in conclusion.

Something especially important happens to children between the ages of nine and ten. Speaking in an abstract way it can be said that children learn to differentiate themselves from their environment; children feel themselves as an "I," and the environment as something external that does not belong to this "I." But this is an abstract way of expressing it. The reality is that, speaking of course in a general sense: the child of this age approaches you with some problem or difficulty. In most cases the child will not actually speak of what is burdening its soul, but will say something different. All the same you have to know this really comes from the innermost depths of the child's soul, and then you must then find the right approach, the right answer. An enormous amount depends on this for the whole future life of the child concerned. For you cannot work with children of this age, as their teacher, unless you are yourself the unquestioned authority, unless, that is, the children have the feeling: this is true because you hold it to be true, this is beautiful because you find it beautiful, and this is good because you think it good—and therefore you are pointing these things out. You must be for the children the representative of the good, the true, and the beautiful. The children must be drawn to truth, goodness, and beauty simply because the children are drawn to you yourself.

And then between the ninth and tenth year a feeling arises instinctively in the child's subconsciousness: I get everything from my teacher, but where does my teacher get it from? What is behind my teacher? If you then go into definitions and explanations it will only do harm. It is important to find a loving word, a word filled with warmth of heart—or rather many words, for these difficulties can go on for weeks and months— so that you can avert this danger and preserve the child's confidence in your authority. For the child has now come to a crisis regarding the principle of authority. If you can meet the situation and can preserve your authority by the warmth of feeling with which you deal with these particular difficulties, if you can meet the child with inner warmth, sincerity, and truth, then much will be gained. The child will retain its belief in your authority, and that is good for the child's further education, but it is also essential that just at this age between nine and ten the child's belief in a good person does not waver. Were this to happen then the inner security that should be the child's guide through life will totter and sway.

This is of very great significance and must constantly be remembered. In handbooks on education you find all kinds of intricate details laid down for the guidance of teachers, but it is of far greater importance to know what happens at a certain point in a child's life and how you should act with regard to it, so that through your action you may radiate light onto the child's whole life.

3

Today we will characterize certain general principles of the art of education for the period between the change of teeth and puberty, passing on in the next lecture to more detailed treatment of single subjects and particular conditions that may arise.

When children reach the ninth or tenth year they begin to differentiate themselves from the environment. For the first time there is a difference between subject and object; subject is what belongs to oneself, object is what belongs to another person or thing. Now you can begin to speak of external things as such, whereas before this time you needed to treat them as though these external objects formed one whole together with the child's own body. I showed yesterday how you could speak of animals and plants, for instance, as though they were human beings who speak and act. The children thereby could have the feeling that the outside world is simply a continuation of their own being.

When children have turned nine or ten you must introduce certain elementary facts of the outside world, the facts of the plant and animal kingdoms. Other subjects I shall speak of later. But it is particularly in this realm that you must be guided by what the children's own nature needs and asks.

The first thing you have to do is to dispense with all the textbooks. For textbooks as they are written at the present time contain nothing about the plant and animal kingdoms that we can use in teaching. They are good for instructing grown-up people about plants and animals, but you will ruin the individuality of the child if you use them at school. And indeed there are no textbooks or handbooks today that show how these things should be taught. Now this is the important point.

If you put single plants in front of the child and demonstrate different things from them, you are doing something that has no reality. A plant by itself is not a reality. If you pull out a hair and examine it as though it were a thing by itself, that would not be a reality either. In ordinary life we say of everything of which we can see the outlines with our eyes that it is real. But if you look at a stone and form some opinion about it, that is one thing; if you look at a hair or a rose, it is another. In ten years' time the stone will be exactly as it is now, but in two days the rose will have changed. The rose is only a reality together with the whole rosebush. The hair is nothing in itself, but is only a reality when considered with the whole head, as part of the whole human being. If you go out into the fields and pull up plants, it is as though you had torn out the hair of the earth. For the plants belong to the earth just in the same way as the hair belongs to the organism of the human being. And it is senseless to examine a hair by itself as though it could suddenly grow anywhere of its own accord.

It is just foolish to take a botanical tin and bring home plants to be examined by themselves. This has no relation to reality, and such a method cannot lead one to a right knowledge of nature or of the human being.

Here we have a plant (see drawing) but this alone is not the plant, for the soil beneath it also belongs to the plant, spread out on all sides and maybe a very long way. There are some plants that send out little roots a very long way. And when you realize that the small clod of earth containing the plant belongs to a much greater area of soil around it, then you will see how necessary it is to manure the earth in order to promote healthy plant growth.

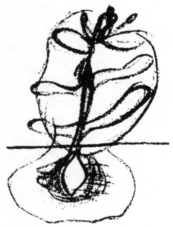

Something else is living besides the actual plant; this part here (below the line in drawing) lives with it and belongs to the plant; the earth lives with the plant.

There are some plants that blossom in the spring, about May or June, and bear fruit in autumn. Then they wither and die and remain in the earth that belongs to them. But there are other plants that take the earth forces out of their environment. If this is the earth, then the root takes into itself the forces around it, and because it has done so these forces shoot upward and a tree is formed.

For what is actually a tree? A tree is a colony of many plants. And it does not matter whether you are considering a hill that has less life in itself but that has many plants growing on it, or a tree trunk where the living earth itself has as it were withdrawn into the tree. Under no circumstances can you understand any plant properly if you examine it by itself.

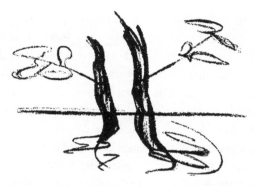

If you go (preferably on foot) into a district where there are definite geological formations, let us say red sand, and look at the plants there, you will find that most of them have reddish-yellow flowers. The flowers belong to the soil. Soil and plant make up a unity, just as your head and your hair also make a unity.

Therefore you must not teach geography and geology by themselves, and then botany separately. That is absurd. Geography must be taught together with a description of the country and observation of the plants, for the earth is an organism and the plants are like the hair of this organism. Children must be able to see that the earth and the plants belong together, and that each portion of soil bears those plants that belong to it.

Thus the only right way is to speak of the plants in connection with the earth, and to give the children a clear feeling that the earth is a living being that has hair growing on it. The plants are the hair of the earth. People speak of the earth as having the force of gravity. This is spoken of as belonging to the earth. But the plants with their force of growth belong to the earth just as much. The earth and the plants are no more separate entities than a person and his or her hair would be. They belong together just as the hair on the head belongs to the person.

If you show children plants out of a botanical tin and tell them their names, you will be teaching something quite unreal. This will have consequences for their whole life, for this kind of plant knowledge will never give them an understanding, for example, of how the soil must be treated, and of how it must be manured, made living by the manure that is put into it. Children can only understand how to cultivate the land if they know how the soil is really part of the plant. People today have less and less conception of reality, the so-called "practical" people least of all, for they are really all theoretical as I showed you in our first lecture, and because they have no longer any idea of reality they look at everything in a disintegrated, isolated way.

Thus it has come about that in many districts during the last fifty or sixty years all agricultural products have become decadent. Not long ago there was a conference on agriculture in central Europe where the agriculturists themselves admitted that crops are now becoming so poor that there is no hope of their being suitable for human consumption in fifty years' time.

Why is this so? It is because people do not understand how to make the soil living by means of manure. It is impossible that they should understand it if they have been given conceptions of plants as being something in themselves, apart from the earth. The plant is no more an object in itself than a hair is. For if this were so, you might expect it to grow just as well in a piece of wax or tallow as in the skin of the head. But it is only in the head that it will grow.

In order to understand how the earth is really a part of plant life you must find out what kind of soil each plant belongs to; the art of manuring can only be arrived at by considering earth and plant world as a unity, and by looking upon the earth as an organism and the plant as something that grows with this organism.

Thus children feel from the very start that they are standing on a living earth. This is of great significance for their whole life. For think what kind of conception people have today of the origin of geological strata. They think of it as one layer deposited upon another. But what you see as geological strata is only hardened plants, hardened living matter. It is not only coal that was formerly a plant (having its roots more in water, rather than in firm ground and belonging completely to the earth) but also granite, gneiss, and so on were originally of plant and animal nature.

This too one can understand only by considering earth and plants as one whole. And in these things it is not only a question of giving children knowledge but of giving them also the right feelings about it. You come to see that this is so when you consider such things from the point of view of Spiritual Science.

You may have the best will in the world. You may say to yourself that the child must learn about everything, including plants, by examining them, and at an early age encourage the child to bring home a nice lot of plants in a beautiful tin box. You examine them together because here is something real. You firmly believe that this is a reality, for it is, after all, an object lesson, but all the time you are looking at something that is not a reality at all. This kind of object-lesson teaching of the present day is utter nonsense.

This way of learning about plants is just as unreal as though it were a matter of indifference whether a hair grew in wax or in the human skin. It cannot grow in wax. Ideas of this kind are completely contradictory to what the child received in spiritual worlds before it descended to the earth. For there the earth looked quite different. This intimate relationship between the mineral earth kingdom and the plant world was then something that the child's soul could receive as a living picture. Why is this so? It is because, in order for human beings to incarnate at all, they have to absorb something that is not yet mineral but is only on the way to becoming mineral, namely the etheric element. The child has to grow into the element of the plants, and this plant world appears to the child as related to the earth.

This series of feelings that children experience when they descend from the pre-earthly world into the earthly world—this whole world of richness—is made confused and chaotic if it is introduced by the usual kind of botany teaching, whereas children rejoice inwardly if they hear about the plant world in connection with the earth.

Similarly we should consider how to introduce our children to the animal world. Even a superficial glance will show us that the animal does not belong to the earth. It runs over the earth and can be in this place or that, so the relationship of the animal to the earth is quite different from that of the plant. Something else strikes us about the animal.

When we come to examine the different animals that live on the earth, let us say according to their soul qualities first of all, we find cruel beasts of prey, gentle lambs, and animals of courage. Some of the birds are brave fighters and we find courageous animals among the mammals, too. We find majestic beasts, like the lion. In fact, there is the greatest variety of soul qualities, and we characterize each single species of animal by saying that it has this or that quality. We call the tiger cruel, for cruelty is its most important and significant quality. We call the sheep patient. Patience is its most outstanding characteristic. We call the donkey lazy, because although in reality it may not be so very lazy, yet its whole bearing and behavior somehow reminds us of laziness. The donkey is especially lazy about changing its position in life. If it happens to be in a mood to go slowly, nothing will induce it to go quickly. And so every animal has its own particular characteristics.

But we cannot think of human beings in this way. We cannot think of one person as being only gentle and patient,
another only cruel, and a third only brave. We should find it a
very one-sided arrangement if people were distributed over the
earth in this way. You do sometimes find such qualities developed in a one-sided way, but not to the same extent as in animals. Rather what we find with human beings, especially when
we are to educate them, is that there are certain things and facts
of life that they must meet with patience or again with courage,
and other things and situations even maybe with a certain cruelty—although cruelty should be administered in homeopathic
doses. Or in certain situations people may show cruelty simply
out of their own natural development, and so on.

Now what is really the truth about these soul qualities of
humans and animals? With humans we find that they can
really possess all qualities, or at least the sum of all the qualities
that the animals have between them (each possessing a different one). Humans have a little of each one. They are not as
majestic as the lion, but they have something of majesty within
them. They are not as cruel as the tiger but they have a certain
cruelty. They are not as patient as the sheep, but they have
some patience. They are not as lazy as the donkey—at least
everybody is not—but they have some of this laziness in them.
All human beings have these things within them. When we
think of this matter in the right way we can say that human
beings have within them the lion-nature, sheep-nature, tiger-
nature, and donkey-nature. They bear all these within them,
but harmonized. All the qualities tone each other down, as it
were, and the human being is the harmonious flowing together,
or, to put it more academically, the synthesis of all the different
soul qualities that the animal possesses. The goal of the human
being is to have the proper dose of lion-ness, sheep-ness, tiger-
ness, donkey-ness, and so on; for all of these to be present in

the right proportions and in the right relationship to everything else.

A beautiful old Greek proverb says: If courage be united with
cleverness it will bring thee blessing, but if it goes alone ruin will
follow. If I were only courageous with the courage of certain
birds that are continually fighting, I would not bring much
blessing into my life. But if my courage is so developed in my
life that it unites with cleverness—the cleverness that in the animal is only one-sided—then it takes its right place in my being.

With the human being, then, it is a question of a synthesis, a
harmonizing of everything that is spread out in the animal
kingdom. We can express it like this: here is one kind of animal
(I am representing it diagrammatically), here a second, a third,
a fourth, and so on, all the possible kinds of animals on the
earth. How are they related to the human being?

The relationship is such that the human being has, let us say,
something of this first kind of animal (see drawing), but modified, not in its entirety. Then comes another kind, but again not
the whole of it. This leads us to the next, and to yet another, so
that all animals are contained within the human being. The animal kingdom is the human being spread out, and the human
being is the animal kingdom drawn together; all the animals are
united synthetically in the human being, and if you analyze a
human being you get the whole animal kingdom.

This is also the case with the external human form. Imagine
a human face and cut away part of it here (see drawing) and
pull another part forward here, so that this latter part is not
harmonized with the whole face, while the forehead recedes;

then you get a dog's head. If you form the head in a somewhat different way, you get a lion's head, and so on.

And so with all the other organs you can find that the human being's external figure has in a modified harmonized form what is distributed among the animals.

Think for instance of a waddling duck; you have a relic of this waddling part between your fingers, only shrunken. Thus everything that is to be found in the animal kingdom even in external form is present also in the human kingdom. Indeed this is the way humans can find their relationship to the animal kingdom, by coming to know that the animals, taken all together, make up the human being. Human beings exist on earth, eighteen hundred million of them, of greater or less value, but they exist again as a giant human being. The whole animal kingdom is a giant human being, not brought together in a synthesis but analyzed out into single examples.

It is as though you were made of elastic that could be pulled out in varying degrees in different directions; if you were thus stretched out in one direction more than in others, one kind of animal would be formed. Or again if the upper part of your face were to be pushed up and stretched out (if it were sufficiently elastic) then another animal would arise. Thus humans bear the whole animal kingdom within them.

This is how the history of the animal kingdom used to be taught in ancient times. This was a right and healthy knowledge, which has now been lost, though only comparatively recently. In the eighteenth century, for instance, people still knew that if the olfactory nerve of the nose is sufficiently large and extended backward then it is a dog's nose. But if the olfactory nerve is shriveled up and only a small portion remains, the rest of it being metamorphosed, then there arises the nerve that we need for our intellectual life.

For observe how a dog smells; the olfactory nerve is extended backward from the nose. A dog smells the special peculiarity of each thing. A dog does not make a mental picture of it, but everything comes to it through smell. A dog has not will and imagination, but has will and a sense of smell for everything. A wonderful sense of smell! A dog does not find the world less interesting than a human does. A human can make mental images of it all, a dog can smell it all. We experience various smells, do we not, both pleasant and unpleasant, but a dog has many kinds of smell—just think how a dog specializes in the sense of smell. Nowadays we have police dogs. They are led to the place where something has been stolen. The dog immediately takes up the scent, follows it, and finds the person. All this is possible because there is really an immense variety, a whole world of scents for a dog and the olfactory nerve carries these scents backward into the head, into the skull.

If we were to draw the olfactory nerve of a dog, which passes through its nose, we should have to draw it going backward. In the human being only a little piece at the bottom of it has remained. The rest of it has been metamorphosed and is here below the forehead. It is a metamorphosed, transformed olfactory nerve, and with this organ we form our mental images. For this reason we cannot smell like a dog, but we can make mental pictures. We bear within us the dog with its sense of smell, only this latter has been transformed into something else. And so it is with all animals.

Let me make this clearer. There is a German philosopher, Schopenhauer, who wrote a book called The World as Will and Idea. This book is only intended for human beings. If it had been written by a dog of genius it would have been called "The World as Will and Smell," and I am convinced that this book would have been much more interesting than Schopenhauer's.

You must look at the various forms of animals and describe them, not as though each animal existed in isolation, but so that you always arouse in the children the thought: This is a picture of the human being. If you think of a human being altered in one direction or another, simplified or combined, then you have an animal. If you take a lower animal, for example, a tortoise form, and put it on the top of a kangaroo, then you have something like a hardened head on the top, for that is the tortoise form, and the kangaroo below stands for the limbs of the human being.

And so everywhere in the wide world you can find some connection between human beings and animals.

You are laughing now about these things. That does not matter at all. It is quite good to laugh about them in the lessons also, for there is nothing better you can bring into the classroom than humor, and it is good for the children to laugh too, for if they always see the teacher come in with a terribly long face they will be tempted to make long faces themselves and to imagine that is what a person has to do when sitting at a desk in a classroom. But if humor is brought in and you can make the children laugh, this is the very best method of teaching. Teachers who are always solemn will never achieve anything with the children.

So here you have the principle of the animal kingdom as I wished to put it before you. We can speak of the details later if we have time. But from this you will see that you can teach about the animal kingdom by considering it as a human being spread out into all the animal forms.

This will give the child a very beautiful and delicate feeling. For as I have pointed out to you, children come to know of the plant world as belonging to the earth, and the animals as belonging to themselves. The children grow with all the kingdoms of the earth. They no longer merely stand on the dead ground of the earth, but on the living ground, for they feel the earth as something living. They gradually come to think of themselves standing on the earth as though they were standing on some great living creature, like a whale. This is the right feeling. This alone can lead them to a really human feeling about the whole world.

So regarding the animal, children come to feel that all animals are related to humans, but that humans have something that reaches out beyond them all, for they unite all the animals in themselves. And all this idle talk of the scientists about the human being descending from an animal will be laughed at by people who have been educated in this way. For they will know that humankind unites within itself the whole animal kingdom, the human being is a synthesis of all the single members of it.

As I have said, between the ninth and tenth year human beings come to the point of discriminating between the self as subject and the outer world as object. There is now the distinction between the self and the surrounding world. Up to this time you could only tell fairy stories and legends in which the stones and plants speak and act like human beings, for children did not yet differentiate between self and environment. But now that the differentiation is made, you must bring the children in touch with their environment on a higher level. You must speak of the earth on which we stand in such a way that the children cannot but feel how earth and plant belong together as a matter of course. Then the children will get practical ideas for agriculture and will know, for instance, that the farmer manures the ground because a certain life is needed in it for one particular species of plant. The children will not then take a plant out of a botanical tin and examine it by itself, nor will they examine animals in an isolated way, but will think of the whole animal kingdom as the great analysis of a human being spread out over the whole earth. Thus we come to know ourselves as we stand on the earth as human beings, and how the animals stand in relationship to us.

It is of very great importance that from the tenth year until toward the twelfth year you should awaken these thoughts of plant-earth and animal-person. Thereby the children can take their place in the world in a very definite way, with their whole life of body, soul, and spirit.

All this must be brought through the feelings in an artistic way, for it is through learning to feel how plants belong to the earth and to the soil that children really become intelligent. Thinking will then be in harmony with nature. Through your efforts to show children how we relate to the animal world you demonstrate how the force of will that is in all animals lives also in the human being, but differentiated, in individualized forms suited to human nature. All animal qualities, all feeling of form that is stamped into the animal nature lives in the human being. Human will receives its impulses in this way and human beings thereby take their place rightly in the world according to their own nature.

Why is it that people go about in the world today as though they had lost their roots? Anyone can see that people do not walk properly nowadays; they do not step properly but drag their legs after them. They learn differently in their sports, but there again there is something unnatural about it. But above all they have no idea how to think nor what to do with their lives. They know well enough what to do if you put them in front of a sewing machine or a telephone, or if an excursion or a world tour is being arranged. But they do not know what to do out of themselves because their education has not led them to find their right place in the world. You cannot put this right by coining phrases about educating people rightly; you can do it only if in the concrete details you can find the right way of speaking of the plants in their true relationship to the soil and of the animals in their rightful place by the side of humankind. Then human beings will stand on the earth as they should and will have the right attitude toward the world. This must be achieved in all your lessons. It is not only important, it is essential.

It will always be a question of finding out what child development demands at each age of life. For this you need real observation and knowledge of the human being. Think once again of the two things that I have discussed, and you will see that children up to their ninth or tenth year are really demanding that the whole world of external nature be made alive, because children do not yet see themselves as separate from this external nature; therefore we tell them fairy tales, myths, and legends. We invent something ourselves for the things that are in our immediate environment, in order that in the form of stories, descriptions, and pictorial representations of all kinds we may give children in an artistic form what is found within their own soul, in the hidden depths that children bring with them into the world. And then after the ninth or tenth year, let us say between the tenth and twelfth year, we introduce children to the animal and plant world as has been described.

We must be perfectly clear that the conception of causality, of cause and effect, that is so popular today has no place at all in what children need to understand even at this age, at the tenth or eleventh year. We are accustomed these days to consider everything in its relation to cause and effect. The education based on natural science has brought this about. But to talk to children under eleven or twelve about cause and effect, as is the practice in the everyday life of today, is like talking about colors to someone who is color blind. You will be speaking entirely beyond children if you speak of cause and effect in the style that is customary today. First and foremost children need living pictures where there is no question of cause and effect. Even after the tenth year these conceptions should only be brought to them in the form of pictures.

It is only toward the twelfth year that children are ready to hear about causes and effects. And so those branches of knowledge that have principally to do with cause and effect in the sense of the words used today—the lifeless sciences such as physics, and so forth—should not be introduced into the curriculum until between the eleventh and twelfth year. Before then one should not speak to the children about mineralogy, physics, or chemistry. None of these things is suitable before this age.

Now regarding history, up to the twelfth year the child should be given pictures of single personalities and well-drawn graphic accounts of events that make history come alive, not a historical review where what follows is always shown to be the effect of what has gone before, the pragmatic method of regarding history, of which our culture has become so proud. This pragmatic method of seeking causes and effects in history is no more comprehensible to the child than colors to the colorblind. And moreover one gets a completely wrong conception of life as it runs its course if one is taught everything according to the idea of cause and effect. I should like to make this clear to you in a picture.

Imagine a river flowing along like this (see drawing).

It has waves. But it would not always be a true picture if you make the wave (C) come out of the wave (B), and this again out of the wave (A), that is, if you say that C is the effect of B and B of A; there are in fact all kinds of forces at work below, which throw these waves up. So it is in history. What happens in 1910 is not always the effect of what happened in 1909, and so on. But quite early on children ought to have a feeling for the things that work in evolution out of the depths of the course of time, a feeling of what throws the waves up, as it were. But they can get that feeling only if you postpone the teaching of cause and effect until later on, toward the twelfth year, and up to this time give them only pictures.

Here again this makes demands on the teachers' fantasy. But teachers must be equal to these demands, and they will be so if they have acquired a knowledge of the human being. This is the one prerequisite.

You must teach and educate out of the very nature of the human being, and for this reason education for moral life must run parallel to the actual teaching that I have been describing to you. So now in conclusion I would like to add a few remarks on this subject, for here too we must read from children's own nature how they should be treated. If you give children of seven a conception of cause and effect you are working against the development of their human nature, and punishments also are often opposed to the real development of their nature.

In the Waldorf School we have had some very gratifying experiences of this. What is the usual method of punishment in schools? A child has done something badly and consequently is required to "stay in" and do some arithmetic for instance. Now in the Waldorf School we once had rather a strange experience: three or four children were told that they had done their work badly and must therefore stay in and do some sums. Whereupon the others said: "But we want to stay and do sums too!"

For they had been brought up to think of arithmetic as something nice to do, not as something that is used as a punishment. You should not arouse in the children the idea that staying in to do sums is something bad, but that it is a good thing to do. That is why the whole class wanted to stay and do sums. So you must not choose punishments that cannot be regarded as such if the children are to be educated in a healthy way in their soul life.

To take another example: Dr. Stein, a teacher at the Waldorf School, often thought of very good educational methods on the spur of the moment. He once noticed that his pupils were passing notes under the desk. They were not attending to the lesson, but were writing notes and passing them under their desks to their neighbors who then wrote notes in reply. Now Dr. Stein did not scold them for writing notes and say: "I shall have to punish you," or something of that sort, but quite suddenly he began to speak about the postal system and give them a lecture on it. At first the children were quite mystified as to why they were suddenly being given a lesson on the postal system, but soon they realized why it was being done. This subtle method of changing the subject made the children feel ashamed. They began to feel ashamed of themselves and stopped writing notes simply on account of the thoughts about the postal system that the teacher had woven into the lesson.

Thus to take charge of a class requires inventiveness. Instead of simply following stereotyped traditional methods you must actually be able to enter into the whole being of the child, and you must know that in certain cases improvement, which is really what we are aiming at in punishment, is much more likely to ensue if the children are brought to a sense of shame in this way without drawing special attention to it or to any one child; this is far more effective than employing some crude kind of punishment. If teachers follow such methods they will

stand before the children actively in spirit, and much will be
balanced out in the class that would otherwise be in disorder.

The first essential for a teacher is self-knowledge. For
instance, if a child blots its book or its desk because of impa-
tience or anger with something a neighbor did, the teacher
must never shout at the child for making blots and say: "You
must not get angry! Getting angry is something a good person
never does! A person should never get angry but should bear
everything calmly. If I see you getting angry once more, why
then—then I shall throw the inkpot at your head!"

If you educate like this (which is very often done) you will
accomplish very little. Teachers must always keep themselves in
hand, and above all must never fall into the faults that they are
blaming the children for. But here you must know how the
unconscious part of the child's nature works. A person's conscious intelligence, feeling, and will are all only one part of the
soul life; in the depths of human nature, even in the child,
there holds sway the astral body with its wonderful prudence
and wisdom.[1]

Now it always fills me with horror to see a teacher standing
in class teaching out of a book, or constantly referring to a
notebook containing questions to ask the children. The children do not appear to notice this consciously, it is true; but if
you are aware of these things then you will see that they have
subconscious wisdom and say to themselves: My teacher does
not know what I am supposed to be learning. Why should I
learn what my teacher does not know? This is always the judgment that is passed by the subconscious nature of children who
are taught by their teacher out of a book.

---

1. For an elucidation of the "astral body" and other higher members of the
human being, see Rudolf Steiner: *The Education of the Child in the Light of
Anthroposophy.*

Such are the imponderable and subtle things that are so extremely important in teaching. For as soon as the subconscious of the child, the astral nature, notices that the teacher does not know something that is being taught, but has to look it up in a book first, then the child considers it unnecessary to learn it either. And the astral body works with much more certainty than the upper consciousness of the child.

These are the thoughts I wished to include in today's lecture. In the next few days I will deal with special subjects and stages in the child's education.

4

TORQUAY / AUGUST 15, 1924

I have shown you how you should teach with descriptive, imaginative pictures between the change of teeth and the ninth or tenth year, for what the children then receive from you will live on in their minds and souls as a natural development, right through their whole lives.

This of course is possible only if the feelings and ideas you awaken are not dead but living. To do this first of all you yourselves must acquire a feeling for the inward life of the soul. Teachers and educators must be patient with their own self-education, with awakening something in the soul that indeed may sprout and grow. You then may be able to make the most wonderful discoveries, but if this is to be so you must not lose courage in your first endeavors.

For you see, whenever you undertake a spiritual activity, you always must be able to bear being clumsy and awkward. People who cannot endure being clumsy and doing things stupidly and imperfectly at first never really will be able to do them perfectly in the end out of their own inner self. And especially in education first of all you must kindle in your own souls what you then have to work out for yourselves; but first it must be enkindled in the soul. If once or twice you have succeeded in thinking out a pictorial presentation of a lesson that you see impresses the children, then you will make a remarkable discovery about yourself. You will see that it becomes easier to invent such pictures, that by degrees you become inventive in a way you had never dreamed of. But for this you must have the courage to be very far from perfect to begin with.

Perhaps you will say you ought never to be a teacher if you have to appear before the children in this awkward manner. But here indeed the anthroposophical outlook must help you along. You must say to yourself: Something is leading me karmically to the children so that I can be with them as a teacher though I am still awkward and clumsy. And those before whom it behooves me not to appear clumsy and awkward—those children—I shall only meet in later years, again through the workings of karma.[1] Teachers and educators thus must take up their lives courageously, for in fact the whole question of education is not a question of the teachers at all but of the children.

Let me therefore give you an example of something that can sink into the child's soul so that it grows as the child grows, something that you can come back to in later years and use to arouse certain feelings. Nothing is more useful and fruitful in teaching than to give the children something in picture form between the seventh and eighth years, and later, perhaps in the fourteenth and fifteenth years, to come back to it again in some way or other. Just for this reason we try to let the children in the Waldorf School remain as long as possible with one teacher. When they come to school at seven years of age the children are given over to a teacher who then takes the class as far as possible, for it is good that things that at one time were given to the children in germ can again and again furnish the content of the methods used in their education.

---

1. Dr. Steiner retained the ancient oriental word "karma" in speaking of the working of human destiny in repeated lives on earth. See Rudolf Steiner: *Theosophy*, chap. 2.

Now suppose for instance that we tell an imaginative story to a child of seven or eight. The child does not need to understand at once all the pictures contained in the story; I will describe later why this is not necessary. All that matters is that the child takes delight in the story because it is presented with a certain grace and charm. Suppose I were to tell the following story:

Once upon a time in a world where the sun peeped through the branches there lived a violet, a very modest violet under a tree with big leaves. And the violet was able to look through an opening at the top of the tree. As she looked through this broad opening in the treetop the violet saw the blue sky. The little violet saw the blue sky for the first time on this morning, because she had only just blossomed. Now the violet was frightened when she saw the blue sky—indeed she was overcome with fear, but she did not yet know why she felt such great fear. Then a dog ran by, not a good dog, a rather bad snappy dog. And the violet said to the dog: "Tell me, what is that up there, that is blue like me?" For the sky also was blue just as the violet was. And the dog in his wickedness said: "Oh, that is a great giant violet like you and this great violet has grown so big that it can crush you." Then the violet was more frightened than ever, because she believed that the violet up in the sky had got so big so that it could crush her. And the violet folded her little petals together and did not want to look up to the great big violet any more, but hid herself under a big leaf that a puff of wind had just blown down from the tree. There she stayed all day long, hiding in her fear from the great big sky-violet.

When morning came the violet had not slept all night, for she had spent the night wondering what to think of the great blue sky-violet who was said to be coming to crush her. And every moment she was expecting the first blow to come. But it did not come. In the morning the little violet crept out, as she was not in the least tired, for all night long she had only been thinking, and she was fresh and not tired (violets are tired when they sleep, they are not tired when they don't sleep!) and the first thing that the little violet saw was the rising sun and the rosy dawn. And when the violet saw the rosy dawn she had no fear. It made her glad at heart and happy to see the dawn. As the dawn faded the pale blue sky gradually appeared again and became bluer and bluer all the time, and the little violet thought again of what the dog had said, that it was a great big violet and it would come and crush her.

At that moment a lamb came by and the little violet again felt she must ask what that thing above her could be. "What is that up there?" asked the violet, and the lamb said, "That is a great big violet, blue like yourself." Then the violet began to be afraid again and thought she would only hear from the lamb what the wicked dog had told her. But the lamb was good and gentle, and because he had such good gentle eyes, the violet asked again: "Dear lamb, do tell me, will the great big violet up there come and crush me?" "Oh no," answered the lamb, "it will not crush you, that is a great big violet, and his love is much greater than your own love, even as he is much more blue than you are in your little blue form." And the violet understood at once that there was a great big violet who would not crush her, but who was so blue in order that he might have more love, and that the big violet would protect the little violet from everything in the world that might hurt her. Then the little violet felt so happy, because what she saw as blue in the great sky-violet appeared to her as divine Love, which was streaming toward her from all sides. And the little violet looked up all the time as if she wished to pray to the God of violets.

Now if you tell the children a story of this kind they will most certainly listen, for they always listen to such things. But you must tell it in the right mood, so that when the children have heard the story they somehow feel the need to live with it and turn it over inwardly in their souls. This is very important, and it all depends on whether discipline can be maintained in the class through the teacher's own feeling.

That is why when we speak of such things as I have just mentioned, we also must consider this question of keeping discipline. We once had a teacher in the Waldorf School, for instance, who could tell the most wonderful stories, but he did not make such an impression upon the children that they looked up to him with unquestioned love. What was the result? When the first thrilling story had been told the children immediately wanted a second. Then they immediately wanted a third, and the teacher gave in again and prepared a third story for them. And at last it came about that after a time this teacher simply could not prepare enough stories. But we must not be continually pumping into the children like a steam pump; there must be a variation, as we shall hear in a moment, for now we must go further and let the children ask questions; we should be able to see from the children's faces and gestures that they want to ask questions. We allow time for questions, and then talk them over in connection with the story that has just been told.

Thus a little child will probably ask: "But why did the dog give such a horrid answer?" and then in a simple childlike way you will be able to tell the child that this dog is a creature whose task is to watch, who has to bring fear to people, who is accustomed to make people afraid of him, and you will be able to explain why the dog gave that answer.

You can also explain to the children why the lamb gave the answer that he did. After telling the above story you can go on talking to the children like this for some time. Then you will find that one question leads to another and eventually the children will bring up every imaginable kind of question. Your task in all this is to bring into the class the unquestioned authority about which we have still much to say. Otherwise it will happen that while you are speaking to one child the others begin to play pranks and to be up to all sorts of mischief. And if you are then forced to turn round and give a reprimand, you are lost! Especially with the little children one must have the gift of letting a great many things pass unnoticed.

I greatly admired the way one of our teachers handled a situation. A few years ago he had in his class a regular rascal (who has now improved very much). And while the teacher was doing something with one of the children in the front row, the boy leapt out of his seat and gave him a punch from behind. Now if the teacher had made a great fuss the boy would have gone on being naughty, but he simply took no notice at all. On certain occasions it is best to take no notice, but to go on working with the child in a positive way. As a general rule it is very bad indeed to take notice of something that is negative.

If you cannot keep order in your class, if you have not this unquestioned authority (I will speak later about how this is to be acquired), then the result will be just as it was in the other case, when the teacher in question would tell one story after another and the children were always in a state of tension that could not be relaxed, for whenever the teacher wanted to pass on to something else and to relax the tension (which must be done if the children are not eventually to become bundles of nerves), then one child left his seat and began to play, the next also got up and began to sing, a third did some eurythmy, a fourth hit her neighbor and another rushed out of the room, and so there was such confusion that it was impossible to bring them together again to hear the next thrilling story.

Your ability to deal with all that happens in the classroom, the good as well as the bad, will depend on your own mood of soul. You can experience the strangest things in this connection, and it is mainly a question of whether the teacher has sufficient self-confidence.

The teacher must come into the class in a mood of mind and soul that can really find its way into the children's hearts. This can only be attained by knowing your children. You will find that you can acquire the capacity to do this in a comparatively short time, even if you have fifty or more children in the class; you can get to know them all and come to have a picture of them in your mind. You will know each one's temperament, special gifts, outward appearance, and so on.

In our teachers' meetings, which are the heart of the whole school life, the single individualities of the children are carefully discussed, and what the teachers themselves learn from their meetings, week by week, is derived first and foremost from this consideration of the children's individualities. In this way the teachers may perfect themselves. The child presents a whole series of riddles, and out of solving these riddles there will grow the feelings that you must carry into the class. When a teacher is not inwardly permeated by what lives in the children, as is sometimes the case, then the children immediately get up to mischief and begin to fight when the lesson has hardly begun. (I know things are better here but I am talking of conditions in central Europe.) This can easily happen, but it is then impossible to go on with a teacher like this, and you have to get another teacher. With the new teacher the whole class is a model of perfection from the first day!

These things may easily come within your experience; it simply depends on whether the teacher is willing to meditate upon the whole group of children with all their peculiarities every morning. You might think that this would take a whole hour. Indeed, if it did take an hour it would be impossible. But this is not so. In fact it can be done in ten or fifteen minutes. The teacher must gradually develop an inward perception of each child's mind and soul, for this is what will make it possible to see at once what is going on in the class.

To get the right atmosphere for this pictorial storytelling you must above all have a good understanding of the temperaments of the children. This is why the treatment of children according to temperament has such an important place in teaching. And you will find that the best way is to begin by seating the children of the same temperament together. In the first place you have a more comprehensive view knowing that over there are the cholerics, there the melancholics, and here the sanguines. This will also give you a vantage point from which to know the whole class.

The very fact that you do this, that you study the children and seat them according to their temperaments, means that you have done something to yourself that will help you to keep the necessary unquestioned authority in the class. These things usually come from sources you least expect. All teachers and educators must work upon themselves inwardly.

If you put the phlegmatics together they will mutually correct each other, for they will be so bored by one another that they will develop a certain antipathy to their own phlegma, and it will get better and better all the time. The cholerics hit and smack each other and finally they get tired of the blows they get from the other cholerics; and so the children of each temperament rub each other's corners off extraordinarily well when they sit together. But when the teacher speaks to the children, for instance when conversing with them about the story that has just been given, the teacher must develop as a matter of course the instinctive gift of treating each child according to temperament. Let us say that I have a phlegmatic child; if I wish to talk over with such a child a story like the one I have just told, I must come across as even more phlegmatic than the child. With a sanguine child who is always flitting from one impression to another and cannot hold on to any of them, I must try to pass from one impression to the next even more quickly than the child does.

With a choleric child you must try to teach things in a quick emphatic way so that you yourself become choleric, and you will see how in the face of your choler the child's own choleric propensities become repugnant to the child. Like must be treated with like, so long as you do not make yourself ridiculous. Thus you will gradually be able to create an atmosphere in which a story like this is not merely related but can be spoken about afterward.

But you must speak about it before you let the children retell the story. The very worst method is to tell a story and then to say: "Now Edith Miller, you come out and retell it." There is no sense in this; it only has meaning if you talk about it first for a time, either cleverly or foolishly; (you need not always be clever in your classes; you can sometimes be quite foolish, and at first you will mostly be foolish). In this way the children make the thing their own, and then if you like you can get them to tell the story again, but this is of less importance for, indeed, it is not so essential that the children should hold such a story in their memory; in fact, for the age of which I am speaking, namely between the change of teeth and the ninth or tenth year, this hardly comes in question at all. Let the children by all means remember what they can, but what has been forgotten is of no consequence. The training of memory can be accomplished in subjects other than storytelling, as I will describe later.

But now let us consider the following question: Why did I choose a story with this particular content? It was because the thought-pictures that are given in this story can grow with the children. You have all kinds of things in the story that you can come back to later. The violet is afraid because she sees the great big violet above her in the sky. You need not yet explain this to the little child, but later when you are dealing with more complicated teaching matter, and the question of fear comes up, you can recall this story. Things small and great are contained in this story, for indeed things small and great are repeatedly coming up again and again in life and working upon each other. Later on, then, you can come back to this. The chief feature of the early part of the story is the snappish advice given by the dog, and later on the kind loving words of advice uttered by the lamb. And when the child has come to treasure these things and has grown older, how easily then you can lead on from the story you told before to thoughts about good and evil, and about such contrasting feelings that are rooted in the human soul. And even with a much older pupil you can go back to this simple child's story; you can make it clear that we are often afraid of things simply because we misunderstand them and because they have been presented to us wrongly. This cleavage in the feeling life, which may be spoken of later in connection with this or that lesson, can be demonstrated in the most wonderful way if you come back to this story in the later school years.

In the religion lessons too, which will only come later on, how well this story can be used to show how the child develops religious feelings through what is great, for the great is the protector of the small, and one must develop true religious feelings by finding in oneself those elements of greatness that have a protective impulse. The little violet is a little blue being. The sky is a great blue being, and therefore the sky is the great blue God of the violet.

This can be used at various stages in the religion lessons. What a beautiful analogy you can draw later on by showing how the human heart itself is of God. One can then say to the child: "Look, this great sky-violet, the god of the violets, is all blue and stretches out in all directions. Now think of a little bit cut out of it—that is the little violet. So God is as great as the world-ocean. Your soul is a drop in this ocean of God. But as the water of the sea, when it forms a drop, is the same water as the great sea, so your soul is the same as the great God is, only it is one little drop of it."

If you find the right pictures you can work with the child in this way throughout the early years, for you can come back to these pictures again when the child is more mature. But you must find pleasure in this picture-making. And you will see that when, by your own powers of invention, you have worked out a dozen of these stories, then you simply cannot escape them; they come rushing in upon you wherever you may be. For the human soul is like an inexhaustible spring that can pour out its treasures unceasingly as soon as the first impulse has been called forth. But people are so indolent that they will not make the initial effort to bring forth what is there in their souls.

We will now consider another branch of this pictorial method of education. We must remember that with the very little child the intellect that in the adult has its own independent life must not yet really be cultivated, but all thinking should be developed in a pictorial and imaginative way.

Now even with children of about eight years of age you can quite easily do exercises of the following kind. It does not matter if they are clumsy at first. For instance you draw this figure (see drawing a). You must try in all kinds of ways to get the children to feel that this is not complete, that something is lacking. How you do this will of course depend on the individuality of each child. You could for instance say: "Look, this goes down to here (left half) but this only comes down to here (right half, incomplete). But this doesn't look nice, coming right down to here and the other side only so far." Thus you will gradually get the child to complete this figure; the child will get the feeling that the figure is unfinished, and must be completed; finally, the child will add this line to the figure. I will draw it in red; the child could of course do it equally well in white, but I am simply indicating in another color what has to be added. At first the attempts will be extremely clumsy, but gradually through balancing out the forms the child will develop observation that is permeated with thought, and thinking that is permeated with imaginative observation. All of the child's thinking will become imagery.

And when you have succeeded in getting a few children in the class to complete things in this simple way, you can then go further with them. You can draw some such figure as the following (see drawing b left,) and after making the children feel that this complicated figure is unfinished you can induce them to put in what will make it complete (right hand part of drawing b). In this way you can arouse a feeling for form that will help the children to experience symmetry and harmony.

This could be continued still further. You could, for instance, awaken in the children a feeling for the inner laws governing this figure (see drawing c). They would see that in one place the lines come together, and in another they separate. This closing together and separating again is something that you can easily bring to their experience.

c   d

Then you pass over to the next figure (see drawing d). You make the curved lines straight, with angles, and they then have to make the inner line correspond. It will be a difficult task with children of eight, but, especially at this age, it is a wonderful achievement if you can get them to do this with all sorts of figures, even if you have shown it to them beforehand. You should get the children to work out the inner lines for themselves; they must bear the same character as the ones in the previous figure but consist only of straight lines and angles.

This is the way to inculcate in the children a real feeling for form, harmony, symmetry, correspondence of lines, and so on. And from this you can pass over to a conception of how an object is reflected; if this, let us say, is the surface of the water (see drawing e) and here is some object, you must arouse in the children's minds a picture of how it will be in the reflection. In this manner you can lead the children to perceive other examples of harmony to be found in the world.

You can also help the children become skillful and mobile in this pictorial imaginative thinking by saying: "Touch your right eye with you left hand! Touch your right eye with your right hand! Touch your left eye with your right hand! Touch your left shoulder with your right hand from behind! Touch your right shoulder with your left hand! Touch your left ear with your right hand! Touch the big toe of your right foot with your right hand!" and so on. You can thus make the children do all kinds of curious exercises, for example, "Describe a circle with your right hand round the left! Describe a circle with your left hand round the right! Describe two circles cutting each other with both hands! Describe two circles with one hand in one direction and with the other hand in the other direction. Do it faster and faster. Now move the middle finger of your right hand very quickly. Now the thumb, now the little finger."

e

So the children can learn to do all kinds of exercises in a quick alert manner. What is the result? Doing these exercises when children are eight years old will teach them how to think—to think for the rest of their lives. Learning to think directly through the head is not the kind of thinking that will last for life. It makes people "thought-tired" later on. But if, on the other hand, they have to do actions with their own bodies that need great alertness in carrying out, and that need to be thought over first, then later on they will be wise and prudent in the affairs of life, and there will be a noticeable connection between the wisdom of such people in their thirty-fifth or thirty-sixth year and the exercises they did as a child of six or seven. Thus it is that the different epochs of life are connected with each other.

Out of such a knowledge of the human being you must try to work out what you have to bring into your teaching.

Similarly you can achieve certain harmonies in color. Suppose you do an exercise with the child by first of all painting something in red (see drawing a) Now show the child in a feeling way that next to this red surface a green surface would be very harmonious. This of course must be carried out with paints, then it is easier to see. Now you can try to explain to the child that you are going to reverse the process. "I am going to put the green in here inside (see drawing b); what will you put round it?" Then the child will put red round it. By doing such things you will gradually lead to a feeling for the harmony of colors. The child comes to see that first I have a red surface here in the middle and green round it (see former drawing), but if the red becomes green, then the green must become red. It is of enormous importance just at this age, towards the eighth year, to let this correspondence of color and form work upon the children.

a   b

Thus our lessons must all be given a certain inner form, and if such a method of teaching is to thrive, the one thing necessary is—to express it negatively—to dispense with the usual timetable. In the Waldorf School we have so-called "period teaching" and not a fixed timetable. We take one subject for four to six weeks; the same subject is continued during that time. We do not have from 8:00-9:00 arithmetic; 9:00-10:00 reading, 10:00-11:00 writing, but we take one subject that we pursue continuously in the main lesson morning by morning for four weeks, and when the children have gone sufficiently far with that subject we pass on to another. We never alternate by having arithmetic from 8:00-9:00 and reading from 9:00-10:00, but we have arithmetic alone for several weeks, then another subject similarly, according to what it may happen to be. There are, however, certain subjects that I will deal with later that require a regular weekly timetable. But, as a rule, in the so-called "main lessons" we keep very strictly to the method of teaching in periods. During each period we take only one subject, but these lessons can include other topics related to it.

We thereby save the children from what can work such harm in their soul life, namely that in one lesson they have to absorb what is then blotted out in the lesson immediately following. The only way to save them from this is to introduce period teaching.

Many will no doubt object that in this kind of teaching the children will forget what they have learned. This only applies to certain special subjects, for example, arithmetic, and can be corrected by frequent little recapitulations. This question of forgetting is of very little account in most of the subjects, at any rate in comparison to the enormous gain children will have if we concentrate on one subject for a certain period of time.

It is essential that you have some understanding of the real essence of every subject that you teach, so that you do not use things in your teaching that are remote from life itself. Everything that is intimately connected with life can be understood. I could even say that whatever one really understands has this intimate connection with life. This is not the case with abstractions.

Today we find that teachers' ideas are largely abstractions, so that in many respects the teachers themselves are remote from life. This is a source of great difficulties in education and teaching. Just consider the following: Imagine that you want to think over how you first came to count things and what really happens when you count. You will probably find that the thread of your recollections breaks somewhere, and that you did once learn to count, but actually you do not really know what you do when you count.

Now all kinds of theories are thought out for the teaching of numbers and counting, and it is customary to act upon such theories. But even when external results can be obtained, the whole being of the child is not touched with this kind of counting or with similar things that have no connection with real life. The modern age has proved that it lives in abstractions, by inventing such things as the abacus or bead-frame for teaching. In a business office people can use calculating machines as much as they like—that does not concern us at the moment, but in teaching, this calculating machine, which is exclusively concerned with the activities of the head, prevents you from the very start from dealing with numbers in accordance with the child's nature.

Counting however should be derived from life itself, and here it is supremely important to know from the beginning that you should not ever expect a child to understand every single thing you teach. Children must take a great deal on authority, but they must take it in a natural, practical way.

Perhaps you may find that what I am now going to say will be rather difficult for the child. But that does not matter. It is of great significance that there should be moments in a person's life when in the thirtieth or fortieth year one could say to oneself: Now I understand what in my eighth or ninth year, or even earlier, I took on authority. This awakens new life in a person. But if you look at all the object lessons that are introduced into the teaching of today, you may well be in despair over the way things are trivialized, in order, as one says, to bring them nearer to the child's understanding.

Now imagine that you have quite a young child in front of you, one who still moves quite clumsily, and you say: "You are standing there before me. Here I take a piece of wood and a knife, and I cut the wood into pieces. Can I do that to you?" The child will see that I cannot do it. And now I can say: "Look, if I can cut the piece of wood in two, the wood is not like you, and you are not like the wood, for I cannot cut you in two like that. So there is a difference between you and the wood. The difference lies in the fact that you are a unit, a 'one', and the wood is not a 'one'. You are a unit and I cannot cut you in two, and therefore I call you 'one', a unit."

You can now gradually proceed to show the child a sign for this "one". You make a stroke: I, so that you show it is a unit and you make this stroke for it.

Now you can leave this comparison between the wood and the child and you can say: "Look, here is your right hand but you have another hand too, your left hand. If you only had this one hand it could certainly move about everywhere as you do, but if your hand were only to follow the movement of your body you could never touch yourself in the way your two hands can touch each other. For when this hand moves and the other hand moves at the same time, then they can take hold of each other, they can come together. That is different from when you simply move alone. In that you walk alone you are a unit. But the one hand can touch the other hand. This is no longer a unit, this is a duality, a 'two'. See, you are one, but you have two hands." This you then show like this: II.

In this way you can work out a conception of the "one" and the "two" from the child's own form.

Now you call out another child and say: "When you two walk toward each other you can also meet and touch each other; there are two of you, but a third can join you. This is impossible with your hands." Thus you can proceed to the three: III.

In this manner you can derive numbers out of what the human being is itself. You can lead over to numbers from the human being, who is not an abstraction but a living being.

Then you can say: "Look, you can find the number two somewhere else in yourself." The children will think finally of their two legs and feet. Now you say: "You have seen your neighbor's dog, haven't you? Does the dog only go on two feet also?" Then the children will come to realize that the four strokes IIII are a picture of the neighbor's dog propped up on four legs, and thus will gradually learn to build up numbers out of life.

The teacher's eyes must always be alert and look at everything with understanding. Now you naturally begin to write numbers with Roman figures, because the children of course will immediately understand them, and when you have got to the four you will easily be able, with the hand, to pass over to five—V. You will soon see that if you keep back your thumb you can use this four as the dog does!: I I I I. Now you add the thumb and make five=V.

I was once with a teacher who had got up to this point (in explaining the Roman figures) and could not see why it occurred to the Romans not to make five strokes next to one another but to make this sign V for the five. He got on quite well up to I I I I. Then I said: "Now let us do it like this: Let us spread out our fingers and our thumb so that they go in two groups, and there we have it, V. Here we have the whole hand in the Roman five and this is how it actually originated. The whole hand is there within it."

In a short lecture course of this kind it is only possible to explain the general principle, but in this way we can derive the idea of numbers from real life, and only when a number has thus been worked out straight from life should you try to introduce counting by letting the numbers follow each other. But the children should take an active part in it. Before you come to the point of saying: Now tell me the numbers in order, 1,2,3,4,5,6,7,8,9 and so on, you should start with a rhythm; let us say we are going from 1 to 2, then it will be: 1,2; 1,2; 1,2; let the child stamp on 2 and then on to 3 also in rhythm: 1,2,3; 1,2,3. In this way we bring rhythm into the series of numbers, and thereby too we foster the child's faculty of comprehending the thing as a whole. This is the natural way of teaching the children numbers, out of the reality of what numbers are. For people generally think that numbers were thought out by adding one to the other. This is quite untrue, for the head does not do the counting at all. In ordinary life people have no idea what a peculiar organ the human head really is, and how useless it is for our earthly life. It is there for beauty's sake, it is true, because our faces please each other. It has many other virtues too, but as far as spiritual activities are concerned it is really not nearly so much in evidence, for the spiritual qualities of the head always lead back to a person's former earth-life. The head is a metamorphosis of the former life on earth, and the fact of having a head only begins to have a real meaning when we know something of our former earthly lives. All other activities come from somewhere else, not from the head at all. The truth is that we count subconsciously on our fingers. In reality we count from one to ten on our ten fingers, then eleven (adding the toes), twelve, thirteen, fourteen (counting on the toes). You cannot see what you are doing, but you go up to twenty. And what you do in this manner with your fingers and toes only throws its reflection into the head. The head only looks on at all that occurs. The head is really only an apparatus for reflecting what the body does. The body thinks, the body counts. The head is only a spectator.

We can find a remarkable analogy for this human head. If you have a car and are sitting comfortably inside it, you are doing nothing yourself; it is the chauffeur in front who has to exert himself. You sit inside and are driven through the world. So it is with the head; it does not toil and moil, it simply sits on the top of your body and lets itself be carried quietly through the world as a spectator. All that is done in spiritual life is done from the body. Mathematics is done by the body, thinking is also done by the body, and feeling too is done with the body. The bead-frame has arisen from the mistaken idea that reckoning is done with the head. Sums are then taught to the child with the bead-frame, that is to say, the child's head is made to work and then the head passes on the work to the body, for it is the body that must do the reckoning. This fact, that the body must do the reckoning, is not taken into account, but it is important. So it is right to let the children count with their fingers and also with their toes, for indeed it is good to call forth the greatest possible skill in the children. In fact there is nothing better in life than making the human being skillful in every way. This cannot be done through sports, for sports do not really make people skilled. What does make a person skilled is holding a pencil between the big toe and the next toe and learning to write with the foot, to write figures with the foot. This can be of real significance, for in truth a person is permeated with soul and spirit in the whole body. The head is the traveller that sits back restfully inside and does nothing, while the body, every part of it, is the chauffeur who has to do everything.

Thus from the most varied sides you must try to build up what the child has to learn as counting. And when you have worked in this way for a time it is important to pass on and not merely take counting by adding one thing to another; indeed this is the least important aspect of counting and you should now teach the child as follows: "This is something that is ONE. Now you divide it like this, and you have something that is TWO. It is not two ONEs put together but the two come out of the ONE." And so on with three and four. Thus you can awaken the thought that the ONE is really the comprehensive thing that contains within itself the TWO, the THREE, the FOUR, and if you learn to count in the way indicated in the diagram, 1,2,3,4 and so on, then the child will have concepts that are living and thereby come to experience something of what it is to be inwardly permeated with the element of number.

In the past our modern conceptions of counting by placing one bean beside another or one bead beside another in the frame were quite unknown; in those days it was said that the unit was the largest, every two is only the half of it, and so on. So you come to understand the nature of counting by actually looking at external objects. You should develop the child's thinking by means of external things that can be seen, and keep as far away as possible from abstract ideas.

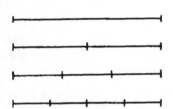

The children can then gradually learn the numbers up to a certain point, first, let us say, up to twenty, then up to a hundred and so on. If you proceed on these lines you will be teaching them to count in a living way. I should like to emphasize that this method of counting, real counting, should be presented before the children learn to do sums. They ought to be familiar with this kind of counting before you go on to arithmetic.

Arithmetic too must be drawn out of life. The living thing is always a whole and must be presented as a whole first of all. It is wrong for children to have to put together a whole out of its parts, when they should be taught to look first at the whole and then divide this whole into its parts; get them first to look at the whole and then divide it and split it up; this is the right path to a living conception.

Many of the effects of our materialistic age on the general culture of humankind pass unnoticed. Nowadays, for instance, no one is scandalized but regards it rather as a matter of course to let children play with boxes of bricks, and build things out of the single blocks. This of itself leads them away from what is living. There is no impulse in the child's nature to put together a whole out of parts. The child has many other needs and impulses that are, admittedly, much less convenient. If you give a child a watch for instance, the child's immediate desire is to pull it to pieces, to break up the whole into its parts, which is actually far more in accordance with human nature—to see how the whole arises out of its components.

This is what must now be taken into account in our arithmetic teaching. It has an influence on the whole of culture, as you will see from the following example.

In the conception of human thought up to the thirteenth and fourteenth centuries very little emphasis was placed upon putting together a whole out of its parts; this arose later. Master-builders built much more from the idea of the whole (which they then split up into parts) rather than starting with the single parts and making a building out of these. The latter procedure was really only introduced into civilization later on. This conception then led to people thinking of every single thing as being put together out of the very smallest parts. Out of this arose the atomic theory in physics, which really only comes from education. For atoms are really tiny little caricatures of demons, and our learned scholars would not speak about them as they do unless people had grown accustomed, in education, to putting everything together out of its parts. Thus it is that atomism has arisen.

We criticize atomism today, but criticism is really more or less superfluous because people cannot get free from what they have been used to thinking wrongly for the last four or five centuries; they have become accustomed to go from the parts to the whole instead of letting their thoughts pass from the whole to the parts.

This is something you should particularly bear in mind when teaching arithmetic. If you are walking toward a distant wood you first see the wood as a whole, and only when you come near it do you perceive that it is made up of single trees.

This is just how you must proceed in arithmetic. You never have in your purse, let us say, 1,2,3,4,5 coins, but you have a heap of coins. You have all five together, which is a whole. This is what you have first of all. And when you cook pea soup you do not have 1,2,3,4,5 or up to 30 or 40 peas, but you have one heap of peas, or with a basket of apples, for instance, there are not 1,2,3,4,5,6,7 apples but one heap of apples in your basket. You have a whole. What does it matter, to begin with, how many you have? You simply have a heap of apples that you are now bringing home (see diagram). There are, let us say, three children. You will not now divide them so that each gets the same, for perhaps one child is small, another big. You put your hand into the basket and give the bigger child a bigger handful, the smaller child a smaller handful; you divide your heap of apples into three parts.

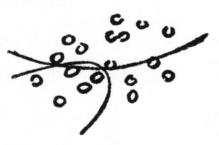

Dividing or sharing out is in any case such a strange business! There was once a mother who had a large piece of bread. She said to her little boy, Henry: "Divide the bread, but you must divide it in a Christian way." Then Henry said: "What does that mean, divide it in a Christian way?" "Well," said his mother, "You must cut the bread into two pieces, one larger and one smaller; then you must give the larger piece to your sister Anna and keep the smaller one for yourself." Whereupon Henry said, "Oh well, in that case let Anna divide it in a Christian way!"

Other conceptions must come to your aid here. We will do it like this, that we give this to one child, let us say (see lines in the drawing), and this heap to the second child, and this to the third. They have already learned to count, and so that we get a clear idea of the whole thing we will first count the whole heap. There are eighteen apples. Now I have to count up what they each have. How many does the first child get? Five. How many does the second child get? Four. And the third? Nine. Thus I have started from the whole, from the heap of apples, and have divided it up into three parts.

Arithmetic is often taught by saying: "You have five, and here is five again and eight; count them together and you have eighteen." Here you are going from the single thing to the whole, but this will give the child dead concepts. The child will not gain living concepts by this method. Proceed from the whole, from the eighteen, and divide it up into the addenda; that is how to teach addition.

Thus in your teaching you must not start with the single addenda, but start with the sum, which is the whole, and divide it up into the single addenda. Then you can go on to show that it can be divided up differently, with different addenda, but the whole always remains the same. By taking addition in this way, not as is very often done by having first the addenda and then the sum, but by taking the sum first and then the addenda, you will arrive at conceptions that are living and mobile. You will also come to see that when it is only a question of a pure number the whole remains the same, but the single addenda can change. This peculiarity of number, that you can think of the addenda grouped in different ways, is very clearly brought out by this method.

From this you can proceed to show the children that when you have something that is not itself a pure number but that contains number within it, as the human being for example, then you cannot divide it up in all these different ways. Take the human trunk for instance and what is attached to it—head, two arms and hands, two feet; you cannot now divide up the whole as you please; you cannot say: now I will cut out one foot like this, or the hand like this, and so on, for it has already been membered by nature in a definite way. When this is not the case, and it is simply a question of pure counting, then I can divide things up in different ways.

Such methods as these will make it possible for you to bring life and a kind of living mobility into your work. All pedantry will disappear and you will see that something comes into your teaching that the child badly needs: humor comes into the teaching, not in a childish but in a healthy sense. And humor must find its place in teaching.[1]

This then must be your method: always proceed from the whole. Suppose you had such an example as the following, taken from real life. A mother sent Mary to fetch some apples. Mary got twenty-five apples. The apple-woman wrote it down on a piece of paper. Mary comes home and brings only ten apples. The fact is before us, an actual fact of life, that Mary got twenty-five apples and only brought home ten. Mary is an honest little girl, and she really didn't eat a single apple on the way, and yet she only brought home ten. And now someone comes running in, an honest person, bringing all the apples that Mary dropped on the way. Now there arises the question: How many does this person bring? We see him coming from a distance, but we want to know beforehand how many he is going to bring. Mary has come home with ten apples, and she got twenty-five, for there it is on the paper written down by the

---

1. At this point Dr. Steiner turned to the translator and said: "Please be sure you translate the word 'humor' properly, for it is always misunderstood in connection with teaching!"

apple-woman, and now we want to know how many this person ought to be bringing, for we do not yet know if he is honest or not. What Mary brought was ten apples, and she got twenty-five, so she lost fifteen apples.

Now, as you see, the sum is done. The usual method is that something is given and you have to take away something else, and something is left. But in real life—you may easily convince yourselves of this—it happens much more often that you know what you originally had and you know what is left over, and you have to find out what was lost. Starting with the minuend and the subtrahend and working out the remainder is a dead process. But if you start with the minuend and the remainder and have to find the subtrahend, you will be doing subtraction in a living way. This is how you may bring life into your teaching.

You will see this if you think of the story of Mary and her mother and the person who brought the subtrahend; you will see that Mary lost the subtrahend from the minuend and that has to be justified by knowing how many apples the person you see coming along will have to bring. Here life, real life, comes into your subtraction. If you say, so much is left over, this only brings something dead into the child's soul. You must always be thinking of how you can bring life, not death, to the child in every detail of your teaching.

You can continue in this way. You can do multiplication by saying: "Here we have the whole, the product. How can we find out how many times something is contained in this product?" This thought has life in it. Just think how dead it is when you say: We will divide up this whole group of people, here are three, here are three more, and so on, and then you ask: how many times three have we here? That is dead, there is no life in it.

If you proceed the other way round and take the whole and ask how often one group is contained within it, then you bring life into it. You can say to the children, for instance: "Look, there is a certain number of you here." Then let them count up; how many times are these five contained within the forty-five? Here again you consider the whole and not the part. How many more of these groups of five can be made? Then it is found out that there are eight more groups of five. Thus, when you do the thing the other way round and start with the whole—the product—and find out how often one factor is contained in it you bring life into your arithmetical methods and above all you begin with something that the children can see before them. The chief point is that thinking must never, never be separated from visual experience, from what the children can see, for otherwise intellectualism and abstractions are brought to the children in early life and thereby ruin their whole being. The children will become dried up and this will affect not only the soul life but the physical body also, causing desiccation and sclerosis. (I shall later have to speak of the education of spirit, soul, and body as a unity.)

Here again much depends on our teaching arithmetic in the way we have considered, so that in old age the human being is still mobile and skillful. You should teach the children to count from their own bodies as I have described, 1,2,3,4,5,6,7,8,9,10, first with the fingers and then with the toes—yes indeed, it would be good to accustom the children actually to count up to twenty with their fingers and toes, not on a bead-frame. If you teach them thus then you will see that through this childlike kind of "meditation" you are bringing life into the body; for when you count on your fingers or toes you have to think about these fingers and toes, and this is then a meditation, a healthy kind of meditating on one's own body. Doing this will allow the grown person to remain skillful of limb in old age; the limbs can still function fully because they have learned to count by using the whole body. If a person only thinks with the head, rather

than with the limbs and the rest of the organism, then later on
the limbs lose their function and gout sets in.

This principle, that everything in teaching and education
must be worked out from what can be seen (but not from what
are often called "object lessons" today)—this principle I should
like to illustrate for you with an example, something that can
actually play a very important part in teaching. I am referring
to the Theorem of Pythagoras that as would-be teachers you
must all be well acquainted with, and that you may even have
already come to understand in a similar way; but I will speak of
it again today. Now the Theorem of Pythagoras can be taken as
a kind of goal in the teaching of geometry. You can build up
your geometry lessons to reach their climax, their summit, in
the Theorem of Pythagoras, which states that the square on the
hypotenuse of a right-angled triangle is equal to the sum of the
squares on the other two sides. It is a marvelous thing if you see
it in the right light.

I once had to teach geometry to an elderly lady because she
loved it so much; she may have forgotten everything, I do not
know, but she had probably not learned much at her school,
one of those schools for the "Education of Young Ladies." At all
events she knew no geometry at all, so I began and made everything lead up to the Theorem of Pythagoras which the old lady
found very striking. We are so used to it that it no longer strikes
us so forcibly, but what we have to understand is simply that if I
have a right-angled triangle here (see diagram) the area of the
square on the hypotenuse is equal to the sum of the other two
areas, the two squares on the other two sides. So that if I am
planting potatoes and put them at the same distance from each
other everywhere, I shall plant the same number of potatoes in
the two smaller fields together as in the larger one. This is something very remarkable, very striking, and when you look at it
like this you cannot really see how it comes about.

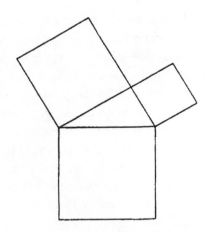

It is just this fact of the wonder of it, that you cannot see how it comes about, that you must make use of to bring life into the more inward, soul quality of your teaching; you must build on the fact that here you have something that is not easily discernible; this must constantly be acknowledged. One might even say with regard to the Theorem of Pythagoras that you can believe it, but you always have to lose your belief in it again. You have to believe afresh every time that this square is equal to the sum of the other two squares.

Now of course all kinds of proofs can be found for this, but the proof ought to be given in a clear visual way. (Dr. Steiner then built up a proof for the Theorem of Pythagoras in detail based on the superposition of areas: he gave it in the conversational style used in this lecture course, and with the help of the blackboard and colored chalks. For those who are interested in a verbatim report of this a proof, with diagrams, can be found in the Appendix on pages 88–90).

If you use this method of proof, that is, laying one area over the other, you will discover something. If you cut it out instead of drawing it you will see that it is quite easy to understand. Nevertheless, if you think it over afterward you will have forgotten it again. You must work it out afresh every time. You cannot easily hold it in your memory, and therefore you must rediscover it every time. That is a good thing, a very good thing. It is in keeping with the nature of the Theorem of Pythagoras. You must arrive at it afresh every time. You should always forget that you have understood it. This belongs to the remarkable quality of the Theorem of Pythagoras itself, and thereby you can bring life into it. You will soon see that if you make your pupils do it again and again, they have to ferret it out by degrees. They do not get it at once, they have to think it out each time. But this is in accordance with the inner living quality of the Theorem of Pythagoras. It is not good to give a proof that can be understood in a flat, dry kind of way; it is much better to forget it again constantly and work it out every time afresh. This is inherent in the very wonder of it, that the square on the hypotenuse is equal to the squares on the other two sides.

With children of eleven or twelve you can quite well take geometry up to the point of explaining the Theorem of Pythagoras by this comparison of areas, and the children will enjoy it immensely when they have understood it. They will be enthusiastic about it, and will always be wanting to do it again, especially if you let them cut it out. There will perhaps be a few intellectual good-for-nothings who remember it quite well and can always do it again. But most of the children, being more reasonable, will cut it out wrong again and again and have to puzzle it out till they discover how it has to go. That is just the wonderful thing about the Theorem of Pythagoras, and you should not forsake this realm of wonder but should remain within it.

APPENDIX TO LECTURE 5

I. *Proof for the Theorem of Pythagoras.*

(As it has been impossible to reproduce the diagrams in color, the forms that Dr. Steiner referred to by their colors have been indicated by letters or numbers.) It is quite easy to do this proof if the triangle is isosceles. If you have here a right-angled isosceles triangle (see diagram *a*), then this is one side, this is the other and this is the hypotenuse. This square (1,2,3,4) is the square on the other two sides.

Now if I plant potatoes evenly in these two fields (2,5) and (4,6), I shall get just as many as if I plant potatoes in this field (1,2,3,4). (1,2,3,4) is the square on the hypotenuse, and the two fields (2,5) and (4,6) are the squares on the other two sides.

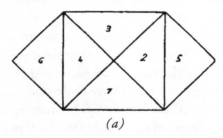

(a)

You can make the proof quite obvious by saying: the parts (2) and (4) of the two smaller squares fall into this space here (1,2,3,4, the square on the hypotenuse); they are already within it. The part (5) exactly fits into the space (3), and if you cut out the whole thing you can take the triangle (6) and apply it to (1), and you will see at once that it is the same. So that the proof is quite clear if you have a so-called right-angled isosceles triangle.

If however you have a triangle that is not isosceles, but has unequal sides (see diagram *b*), you can do it as follows:

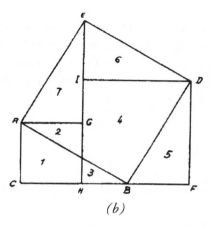

(b)

Draw the triangle again ABC; then draw the square on the hypotenuse ABDE. Proceed as follows: draw the triangle ABC again over here, DBF. Then this triangle ABC or DBF (which is the same), can be put up there, AGE. Since you now have this triangle repeated over there, you can draw the square over one of the other sides CAGH.

As you can see, I can now also draw this triangle DEI congruent to BCA. Then the square DIHF is the square on the other side. Here I have both the square on the one side and the square on the other side. In the one case I use the side AG and in the other case the side DI. The two triangles AEG and DEI are congruent. Where is then the square on the hypotenuse? It is the square ABDE. Now I have to show from the figure itself that (1,2) and (3,4,5) together make up (2,4,6,7). Now I first take the square (1,2); this has the triangle (2) in common with the square on the hypotenuse ABDE and section (4) of the square on the other side HIDF is also contained in ABDE. Thus I get this figure (2,4) which you see drawn here and which is actually a piece of the square ABDE. This only leaves parts (1,3, and 5) of the squares AGHC and DIHF to be fitted into the square on the hypotenuse ABDE.

Now you can take part (5) and lay it over part (6), but you will still have this corner (1,3) left over. If you cut this out you will discover that these two areas (1, 3) fit into this area (7). Of course it can be drawn more clearly but I think you will understand the process.

6

W e will now continue our discussion by speaking of certain matters of method, and here I would like to say that in these few lectures only general principles can be given. You can also study the Waldorf School seminar courses, and with the indications you have received here you will be able to understand them thoroughly. We must get a clear picture of the child between the change of teeth and puberty; we must know that in the years before the change of teeth the inherited characteristics are the determining factors, and that the child receives from its father and mother a "model" body that is completely thrown aside by the time of the change of teeth, for during the first seven-year period it is being replaced by a new body. The change of teeth, indeed, is only the external expression of this replacing of the old body by a new one, upon which the soul and spirit are now at work.

I have already told you that if the spirit-soul is strong, then during the school period from the change of teeth to puberty children may go through great changes regarding the qualities they formerly possessed. If the individuality is weak, the result will be a body that very closely resembles the inherited characteristics, and with the children of school age we will still have to take into account deeply-rooted resemblances to the parents or grandparents.

We must be clear in our minds that the independent activity of the etheric body only really begins at the change of teeth. The etheric body in the first seven years has to put forward all the independent activity of which it is capable to build up the second physical body. Thus, this etheric body is preeminently an inward artist in the child in the first seven years; it is a modeler, a sculptor. And this modeling force, applied to the physical body by the etheric body, becomes free, emancipates itself with the change of teeth at the seventh year. It can then work as an activity of soul.

This is why the child has an impulse to model forms or to paint them. For the first seven years of life the etheric body has been carrying out modeling and painting within the physical body. Now that it has nothing further to do regarding the physical body, or at least not as much as before, it wants to carry its activity outside. If therefore you as teachers have a wide knowledge of the forms that occur in the human organism, and consequently know what kind of forms children like to mold out of plastic material or to paint in color, then you will be able to give them the right guidance. But you yourselves must have a kind of artistic conception of the human organism. It is therefore of real importance for the teacher to try and do some modeling as well, for the teachers' training today includes nothing of this sort. You will see that however much you have learned about the lung or the liver, or let us say the complicated ramifications of the vascular system, you will not know as much as if you were to copy the whole thing in wax or plasticine. For then you suddenly begin to have quite a different kind of knowledge of the organs, of the lung for instance. For as you know you must form one half of the lung differently from the other half; the lung is not symmetrical. One half is clearly divided into two segments, the other into three. Before you learn this you are constantly forgetting which is left and which is right. But when you work out these curious asymmetrical forms in wax or plasticine, then you get the feeling that you could not change round left and right any more than you could put the heart on the right hand side of the body. You also get the feeling that the lung has its right place in the organism with its own particular form, and if you mold it rightly you will feel that it is inevitable for the human lung to come gradually into an upright position in standing and walking. If you model the lung forms of animals you will see or you will feel from the touch that the lung of an animal lies horizontally. And so it is with other organs.

You yourselves therefore should really try to learn anatomy by modeling the organs, so that you can then get the children to model or to paint something that is in no way an imitation of the human body but only expresses certain forms. For you will find that the child has an impulse to make forms that are related to the inner human organism. You may get some quite extraordinary experiences in this respect in the course of your lessons.

We have introduced lessons on simple physiology in the school, and especially in the fourth, fifth, sixth, and seventh grades, as this is obviously an integral part of the Waldorf School method. Our children paint from the very beginning, and from a certain age they also do carving. Now if you simply let the children work freely it is very interesting to see that when you have explained about the human being to them, the lung for instance, then out of themselves they begin to model such forms as the lung or something similar. It is really interesting to see how the child forms things out of its own being. That is why it is essential for you to take up this plastic method, and to find ways and means of making faithful reproductions of the forms of the human organs exactly in wax or plasticine—even, if you like, as our children often do, in mud,

for if you have nothing else that is very good material to work
with.

This is an inner urge, an inner longing of the etheric body, to
be at work in modeling or painting. So you can very easily turn
this impulse and longing to account by deriving the letters of
the alphabet out of the forms that the child paints or models,
for then you will be really molding your teaching out of a
knowledge of the human being. This is what must be done at
this stage.

Now to proceed. The human being consists not only of the
physical body and etheric body, which latter is emancipated
and free at the seventh year, but also of the astral body and ego.
What happens to the astral body of the child between the seventh and fourteenth year? It does not really come to its full
activity till puberty. Only then is it working completely within
the human organism. But while the etheric body between birth
and the change of teeth is in a certain sense being drawn out of
the physical body and becoming independent, the astral body
is gradually being drawn inward between the seventh and fourteenth year, and when it has been drawn right in and is no
longer merely loosely connected with the physical and etheric
bodies but permeates them completely, then the human being
has arrived at the moment of puberty, of sexual maturity.

With the boy one can see by the change of voice that the
astral body is now quite within the larynx, with the girl one can
see by the development of other organs, breast organs and so
on, that the astral body has now been completely drawn in.
The astral body finds its way slowly into the human body from
all sides.

The lines and directions it follows are the nerve fibers. The
astral body comes in along the nerve fibers from without
inward. Here it begins to fill out the whole body from the outer
environment, from the skin, and gradually draws itself together

inside. Before this time it is a kind of loose cloud, in which the child lives. Then it draws itself together, lays firm hold upon all the organs, and if we may put it somewhat crudely, it unites itself chemically with the organism, with all the tissues of the physical and etheric body.

But something very strange happens here. When the astral body presses inwards from the periphery of the body it makes its way along the nerves which then unite in the spine (see drawing).

Above is the head. It also forces its way slowly through the head nerves, crawls along the nerves toward the central organs, toward the spinal cord, bit by bit, into the head, gradually coming in and filling it all out.

What we must chiefly consider in this connection is how the breathing works in with the whole nervous system. Indeed this working together of the breathing with the whole nervous system is something very special in the human organism. As teacher and educator one should have the very finest feeling for it; only then will one be able to teach rightly. Here then the air enters the body, distributes itself, goes up through the spinal column (see drawing), spreads out in the brain, touches the nerve fibers everywhere, goes down again and pursues paths by which it can then be ejected as carbon dioxide. So we find the nervous system being constantly worked upon by the in-breathed air that distributes itself, goes up through the spinal column, spreads out again, becomes permeated with carbon, goes back again and is breathed out.

It is only in the course of the first school period, between the changing of teeth and puberty, that the astral body carries this whole process of breathing, passing along the nerve fibers, right into the physical body. So that during this time when the astral body is gradually finding its way into the physical body with the help of the air breathed in, it is playing upon something that is stretched across like strings of an instrument in the center of the body, that is, upon the spinal column. Our nerves are really a kind of lyre, a musical instrument, an inner musical instrument that resounds up into the head.

This process begins of course before the change of teeth, but at that time the astral body is only loosely connected with the physical body. It is between the change of teeth and puberty that the astral body really begins to play upon the single nerve fibers with the in-breathed air, like a violin bow on the strings.

You will be fostering all this if you give the child plenty of singing. You must have a feeling that while singing the child is a musical instrument, you must stand before your class to whom you are teaching singing or music with the clear feeling: every child is a musical instrument and inwardly feels a kind of well-being in the sound.

For you see, sound is brought about by the particular way the breath is circulated. That is inner music. To begin with, in the first seven years of life, the child learns everything by imitation, but now the child should learn to sing out of the inward joy experienced in building up melodies and rhythms. To show you the kind of inner picture you should have in your mind when you stand before your class in a singing lesson, I should like to use a comparison that may seem a little crude, but which will make clear to you what I mean. I do not know how many of you, but I hope most, have at some time been able to watch a herd of cows who have fed and are now lying in the meadow digesting their food.

This digestive process of a herd of cows is indeed a marvelous thing. In the cow a kind of image of the whole world is present. The cow digests her food, the digested foodstuffs pass over into the blood vessels and lymphatic vessels, and during this whole process of digestion and nourishment the cow has a sensation of well-being which is at the same time knowledge. During the process of digestion every cow has a wonderful aura in which the whole world is mirrored. It is the most beautiful thing one can see, a herd of cows lying in the meadow digesting their food, and in this process of digestion comprehending the whole world. With us human beings all this has sunk into the subconscious, so that the head can reflect what the body works out and sees revealed as knowledge.

We are really in a bad way, we human beings, because the head does not allow us to experience the lovely things that the cows, for example, experience. We should know much more of the world if we could experience the digestive process, for instance. We should then of course have to experience it with the feeling of knowledge, not with the feeling that humans have when they remain in the subconscious in their digestive process. This is simply to make clear what I want to say. I do not wish to imply that we now have to raise the process of digestion into consciousness in our teaching, but I want to show that there is something that should really be present in the child at a higher stage, this feeling of well-being at the inward flow of sound. Imagine what would happen if the violin could feel what is going on within it! We only listen to the violin, it is outside us, we are ignorant of the whole origin of the sound and only hear the outward sense picture of it. But if the violin could feel how each string vibrates with the next one it would have the most blissful experiences, provided of course that the music is good. So you must let the child have these little experiences of ecstasy, so that you really call forth a feeling for music in the whole organism, and you must yourself find joy in it.

Of course one must understand something of the music. But an essential part of teaching is this artistic element of which I have just spoken.

On this account it is essential, for the inner processes of life between the change of teeth and puberty demand it, to give the children lessons in music right from the very beginning, and at first, as far as possible to accustom them to sing little songs, quite empirically without any kind of theory: nothing more than simply singing little songs, but they must be well sung! Then you can use the simpler songs from which the children can gradually learn what melody, rhythm, and beat are and so on; but first you must accustom the children to sing little songs as a whole, and to play a little too as far as that is possible. Unless there is clearly no bent at all in this direction every Waldorf child begins to learn some instrument on entering school; as I say, as far as circumstances allow, each child should learn to play an instrument. As early as possible the children should come to feel what it means for their own musical being to flow over into the objective instrument, for which purpose the piano, which should really only be a kind of memorizing instrument, is of course the worst possible thing for the child. Another kind of instrument should be chosen, and if possible one that can be blown upon. Here one must of course have a great deal of artistic tact and, I was going to say, a great deal of authority too. If you can, you should choose a wind instrument, as the children will learn most from this and will thereby gradually come to understand music. Admittedly, it can be a hair-raising experience when the children begin to blow. But on the other hand it is a wonderful thing in the child's life when this whole configuration of the air, which otherwise is enclosed and held along the nerve-fibers, can now be extended and guided. The human being feels the whole organism being enlarged. Processes that are otherwise only within the organism are carried over into the outside world. A similar thing happens when the child learns the violin, when the actual processes, the music that is within, is directly carried over and the child feels how the music within passes over into the strings through the bow.

But remember, you should begin giving these music and singing lessons as early as possible. For it is of very great importance that you not only make all your teaching artistic, but that you also begin teaching the more specifically artistic subjects— painting, modeling, and music, as soon as the children come to school, and that you see to it that the children really come to possess all these things as an inward treasure.

In the life of the child the point of time that falls between the ninth and tenth year must be very specially kept in mind in the teaching of languages. I have characterized for you this turning point between the ninth and tenth year as the time when children first learn to differentiate between themselves and the environment. Up to this time they have been as one. I have already indicated the right method of teaching for children entering school, but they really should not come to school before the change of teeth; we might say that fundamentally any kind of school teaching before this time is wrong; if we were forced to it by law we must do it, but it is not the right thing from the point of view of artistic education. In a true art of education children should not enter school until the change of teeth. Our first task, as I have shown you, is to begin with something artistic and work out the forms of the letters through art; you should begin with some independent form of art as I have explained to you, and treat everything that has to do with nature in the mood and fashion of fairy tales, legends, and myths, in the way I have described. But for teaching languages it is specially important to consider this period between the ninth and tenth year.

Before this time language teaching must under no circumstances be of an intellectual nature; that is to say it must not include any grammar or syntax. Up to the ninth or tenth year children must learn to speak the foreign language just as they acquire any other habit. Only when they learn to differentiate between the self and the environment can they begin to examine what they themselves bring forth in their speech. It is only then that you can begin to speak of noun, adjective, verb, and so on, not before. Before this time the child should simply speak and be kept to this speaking.

We have a good opportunity for carrying this out in the Waldorf School, because from the beginning of school life the child learns two foreign languages besides the mother tongue.

The children come to school and begin with main lessons in periods, as I have already described; they have the main lesson for the early part of the morning, and then directly after that the little ones have a lesson which for German children is either English or French. In these language lessons we try not to consider the relationship of one language to the other. Up until the point of time I have described to you between the ninth and tenth year, we disregard the fact that a table for instance is called "Tisch" in German and "table" in English, that to eat is "essen" in German and "eat" in English; we connect each language not with the words of another language, but directly with the objects. The child learns to call the ceiling, the lamp, the chair, by their names, whether it is in French or in English. Thus from the seventh to the ninth year we should not attach importance to translation, that is to say rendering a word in one language by a word in another, but the children simply learn to speak in the language, connecting their words with the external objects. Thus, the children do not need to know, or rather do not need to think, of the fact that when they say "table" in English it is called "Tisch" in German, and so on; they do not concern themselves with this at all. This does not occur to the children, for they have not been taught to compare the languages in any way.

In this manner the child learns every language out of the element from which it stems, namely, the element of feeling. Now a language consists, of course, of sounds, and is either the expression of the soul from within, in which case there is a vowel, or else it is the expression of something external and then there is a consonant. But you must feel this first of all. You will not of course pass on to the children exactly what I am saying here, but in the course of your lesson they should actually experience the vowel as something connected with feeling, and the consonant as a copy of something in the outside world. This will happen as a matter of course, for it is part of human nature, and we must not drive out this impulse but rather lead on from it.

For let us think, what is the vowel A(ah)?[1] (This does not belong to the lesson, but is only something you ought to know!) What is A? When the sun rises I stand in admiration before it: Ah! A is always the expression of astonishment, wonder. Or again, a fly settles on my forehead; I say: E (Eh). That is the expression of warding off, doing away with: E. the English

---

1. In these references to A and E the *sounds of Ah and Eh* should be considered, not the names of the letters.

sounds are somewhat differently connected with our feelings, but in every language, English included, we find that the vowel A expresses astonishment and wonder.

Now let us take a characteristic word: roll—the rolling of a ball, for instance. Here you have the R. Who could help feeling that with the R and the L together, the ball *rolls on* (see drawing *a*). R alone would be like this (see drawing *b*):

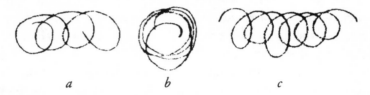

a   b   c

R L goes on. L always implies a flowing on. Here you have an external process imitated in the consonant (see drawing *c*).

So the whole language is built up in the vowels out of a feeling of inner astonishment, wonder, self-defense, self-assertion, and so on, or out of a feeling of imitation in the case of the consonants. We must not drive these feelings out of the children. The children should learn to develop the sounds from the external objects and from the way their own feelings are related to them. Everything should be derived from the feeling for language. In the word "roll" the child should really feel: r,o,l,l. It is the same thing for every word.

This has been completely lost for modern civilized people. They think of the word simply as something written down or something abstract. People can no longer really feel their way into language. Look how all primitive languages still have feeling within them; the most civilized languages make speech an abstract thing. Look at your own English language, how the second half of the word is cast aside, and one skips over the real feeling of the sounds. But the child must dwell in this feeling for language.

This must be cultivated by examining characteristic words in which such a feeling plays. Now in German we call what one has up here "Kopf." In English it is called "head," in Italian "testa." With the abstract kind of relationship to language that people usually have today, what do they say about this? they say, in German the word is "Kopf," in Italian "testa," in English "head." But all this is absolutely untrue. The whole thing is nonsense.

For let us think: "Kopf," what is that? "Kopf" is what is formed, something that has a rounded form. The *form* is expressed when you say "Kopf." When you say "testa"—you have it in the word "testament" and "testify"—then you are expressing the fact that the head establishes or confirms something. Here you are expressing something quite different. You say of that organ that sits up there: that is the establisher, the testator—testa. Now in English one holds the opinion that the head is the most important part of the human being (although you know of course that this opinion is not quite correct). So in English you say "head," that is, the most important thing, the goal of all things, the aim and meeting-place of all.

Thus different things are expressed in the different languages. If people wanted to designate the same thing, then the Englishman and the Italian too would say "Kopf." But they do not designate the same thing. In the primeval human language the same thing was expressed everywhere, so that this primeval language was the same for all. Then people began to separate and to express things differently; that is how the different words came about. When you designate such different things as though they were the same you no longer feel what is contained in them, and it is very important not to drive out this feeling for language. It must be kept alive and for this reason you must not analyze language before the ninth or tenth year.

Only then can you pass on to what a noun, a verb, or an adjective is, and so on: this should not be done before the ninth or tenth year, otherwise you will be speaking of things that are so closely connected with the children's own selves that they cannot understand it yet because they cannot distinguish themselves from their environment. It is most important to bear in mind that we must not allow any grammar or comparison of languages before the ninth or tenth year. Then what the children get from speaking will be similar to what they get from singing.

I have tried to illustrate this inner joy in singing by picturing to you the inner feeling of pleasure that rises up out of the digestive organs of the cows in the meadow when they are digesting their food. There must be present an inner feeling of joy of this kind, or at least some feeling contained in a word, that they feel the inward "rolling." Language must be inwardly experienced and not only thought out with the head. Today you find that people mostly "think" language with their head. Therefore when they want to find the right word in translating from one language to another they take a dictionary. Here the words are so put together that you find "testa" or "Kopf" and people imagine that is all the same. But it is not all the same. A different conception is expressed in each word, something that can only be expressed out of feeling. We must take this into account in language teaching. And another element comes in here, something that belongs to the spirit. When human beings die, or before they come down to earth, they have no possibility of understanding the so-called substantives, for example. Those whom we call the dead know nothing about substantives; they know nothing of the naming of objects, but they still have some knowledge of qualities, and it is therefore possible to communicate with the dead about qualities. But in the further course of the life after death that soon ceases also. What lasts longest is an understanding of verbs, words of action, active and passive expressions, and longest of all the expression of sensations: Oh! Ah! I (ee), E (eh); these interjectional expressions are preserved longest of all by the dead.

From this you can see how vital it is that the human soul have a living experience of interjections if it is not to become entirely un-spiritual. All interjections are actually vowels. And the consonants, which as such are in any case very soon lost after death, and were not present before the descent to earth, are copies of the external world. This we should really experience in our feeling, be aware of it in the child, and see that we do not drive it out by giving lessons on nouns, adjectives, and so on too early, but wait with these until the ninth or tenth year.

From the first class of the Waldorf School upward we have introduced eurythmy, this visible speech in which, by carrying out certain movements either alone or in groups, the human being actually reveals itself just as it reveals itself through speech. Now if there is the right treatment in the language lessons, that is to say if the teacher does not ruin the child's feeling for language but rather cherishes it, then the child will feel the transition to eurythmy to be a perfectly natural one, just as the very little child feels that learning to speak is also a perfectly natural process. You will not have the slightest difficulty in bringing eurythmy to the children. If they are healthily developed children they will want it. You will always discover something that is pathologically wrong with children who do not wish to do eurythmy. They want it as a matter of course, just as when they were quite little children they wanted to learn to speak, if all their organs were sound. That is because the child feels a very strong impulse to express its inward experiences as activities of will in its own body. This can be seen in the very early years when the child begins to laugh and cry, and in the various ways in which feelings are expressed in the face.

It would have to be a very metaphorical way of speaking if you were to say that a dog or any other animal laughs. In any case it does not laugh in the same way the human being does, neither does it cry in the same way. Indeed in the animal all gestures and movements that carry over inward experience into the element of will are quite different. There is a great difference between animal and human in this respect.

What is expressed in eurythmy rests upon laws just as language does. Speaking is not an arbitrary thing. With a word like "water" for instance, you cannot say "vunter," or anything like that. Speech has laws, and so has eurythmy. In the ordinary movements of the body the human being is in a sense free, although many things are done out of a certain instinct. When I cogitate about something, I put my finger to my forehead; when I want to show that something is not true, I shake my head and my hand, as if to erase it. But eurythmy leads inward and outward experiences over into ordered movements, just as speech leads an inward experience over into the sound: this is what eurythmy is, and the child wants to learn it. For this reason the fact that eurythmy is not yet taught in modern education proves that there is no thought of drawing forth the human faculties out of the very nature of the human being, for if you do that then you must come to eurythmy in the natural course of things.

This will not mean any interference with gymnastics, the teaching of physical exercises. This is something quite different, and the teacher and educator must recognize the difference. Gymnastics as taught today and all kinds of sports are something quite different from eurythmy. You can quite well have both together. For the conception of space is very often considered in quite an abstract way, and people do not take into account that space is something concrete. For people have become so accustomed to think of the earth as round that when someone who lives in this part of the world makes a jump he says he jumps "up." But when someone in the Antipodes, who has his legs down here and his head up there, jumps, he jumps "down"—or so we imagine. But this is not anything we can experience. I once read a book on natural philosophy in which the author tried to ridicule the idea that the sky must be below! But the truth is far richer than that. We do not make judgments about the world and about space in such a way that we leave ourselves out of it altogether and simply consider space by itself as something abstract. There are certain philosophers who do this—Hume and Mill and Kant. But this is all untrue. It is really all nonsense. Space is something concrete of which the human being is aware. We each feel ourselves within space and feel the necessity of finding our place in it; when we find our way into the balance of space, into the different conditions of space, then sports and gymnastics arise. With these efforts the human being tries to develop a personal relationship to space.

If you do this gymnastic movement (arms outstretched), you have the feeling that you are bringing your two arms into a horizontal direction. If you jump you have the feeling that you are moving your body upward by its own force. These are gymnastic exercises. But if you feel you are holding within you something that you are experiencing inwardly—the sound EE—and you reflect upon it, then you may make perhaps a similar movement, but in this case, the inner soul quality is expressed in the movement. A person's inward self is revealed. This is what happens in eurythmy, which is the revelation of the inner self. Eurythmy expresses the human experience of breathing and of blood circulation when they come into the realm of the soul. In gymnastics and in sports we feel space as if it were a framework filled with all sorts of lines and directions into which we spring and which we follow, and the apparatus is made accordingly. We climb a ladder or pull ourselves up on a rope. Here we are acting in accordance with external space.

That is the difference between gymnastics and eurythmy. Eurythmy lets the soul life flow outward, and thereby becomes a real expression of the human being, like language; eurythmy is visible speech.

Gymnastics and sports are a way for human beings to fit themselves into external space, adapt themselves to the world, experiment to see whether one fits in with the world in this way or in that. That is not language, that is not a revelation of the human being, but rather a demand the world makes upon human beings so that they should be fit for the world and be able to find their way into it. This difference must be noticed. It expresses itself in the fact that the gymnastics teacher makes the children do movements whereby they may adapt themselves to the outside world. The eurythmy teacher expresses what is the inner nature of the human being. We must feel this, we must be aware of it. Then eurythmy, gymnastics, and games too, if you like, will all take their right place in our teaching.

We will speak further of this tomorrow.

7

We will now speak about some further details of method, though of course in this short time I can only pick out a few examples to give you.

When we consider the whole period between the change of teeth and puberty we can see that it divides itself again into three sections, and we must bear these in mind when we have to guide the children through those early years of school life. First we have the age when children begin to differentiate themselves from their environment and make a distinction between "subject"—their own self, and "object"—the things that surround them in the outside world. Up to this time it is essential for us to teach in such a way that all things inside or outside the child have a quality of unity. I have shown you how that can be done artistically. Then, in the second period, we saw how the transition to descriptions of the outside world can be made through our teaching of plant and animal life. You can treat these things in quite an elementary way up till the twelfth year. The third section extends from the twelfth year up to puberty, and it is really only at this time that we can pass on to lifeless nature, for it is only now that the child really begins to understand the inanimate world.

We might indeed say that from the seventh year to about nine-and-a-half or nine-and-one-third children take everything in with their soul. There is nothing that a child would not take in with its soul. The trees, the stars, the clouds, the stones, everything is absorbed by the child's soul life. From about nine-and-a-third to about eleven-and-two-thirds children already perceive the difference between the soul quality that they see in themselves and what is merely "living." We can now speak of the whole earth as living. Thus we have the soul quality and the living quality. Then from eleven-and-two-thirds to about four-teen the child discriminates between what is of the soul, what is living, and what is dead, that is to say, what is based on the laws of cause and effect. (no will?)

We should not speak to children of inanimate things at all before they approach the twelfth year. Only then should we begin to speak about minerals, physical phenomena, chemical phenomena, and so on. We must make it clear to ourselves that this is really how things are: in the child between the change of teeth and puberty it is not the intellect but the fantasy that is predominantly active; we must constantly be thinking of the child's fantasy, and therefore, as I have often said, we must especially develop fantasy in ourselves. If we do not do this, but pass over to all kinds of intellectual things when the children are still quite young, then they cannot go through their devel-opment rightly even in their physical body. And much that is pathological today arises from the fact that in this materialistic age too much attention has been paid to children's intellect between the change of teeth and puberty.

We should only very gradually introduce the lifeless world when the child is approaching the twelfth year, for this lifeless world must be grasped by the intellect. At this time we can introduce minerals, physical and chemical phenomena, and so on. But even here we should connect it up with life as far as possible, not simply start, for instance, with a collection of minerals, but start from the earth, the soil, and first describe the mountain ranges, how they bring about the configuration of the earth; then we can speak of how the foot of the mountains is surrounded with soil, and the higher we go the more barren the mountains become and the fewer plants there are. So we come to speak of the barrenness of the mountains and point out that here there are minerals. Thus we start with the mountains and lead on to the minerals.

Then when we have given a clear description of the mountains we can show the children a mineral and say: this is what you would find if you were to take this path up the mountain. This is where it is found. When you have done this with a few different minerals you can pass on to speak of the minerals themselves. But you must do the other first, here again proceeding from the whole and not from the part. This is very important.

For physical phenomena also it is just as important to start from life itself. You should not begin your teaching of physics as set forth in the textbooks of today, but simply by lighting a match for instance and letting the children observe how it begins to burn; you must draw their attention to all the details, what the flame looks like, what it is like outside, what it is like further in, and how a black spot, a little black cap is left when you blow out the flame; and when you have done this, begin to explain how the fire in the match came about. The fire came about through the generation of warmth, and so on. Thus you must connect everything with life itself.

Or take the example of a lever: do not begin by saying that a lever consists of a supported beam at the one end of which there is a force, and at the other end another force, as one so often finds in the physics books. You should start from a pair of scales; let the child imagine that you are going to some shop where things are being weighed out, and from this pass on to equilibrium and balance, and to the conception of weight and gravity. Always develop your physics from life itself, and also your chemical phenomena.

That is the essential thing, to begin with real life in considering the different phenomena of the physical and mineral world. If you do it the other way, beginning with an abstraction, then something very curious happens to the children; the lesson itself soon makes them tired. The children do not get tired if you start from real life, they get tired if you start from abstractions.

The golden rule for the whole of teaching is that the children should not tire. Now there is something very strange about the so-called experimental education of the present day. Experimental psychologists register when a child becomes tired in any kind of mental activity, and from this they decide how long to occupy a child with any one subject, in order to avoid fatigue.

This whole conception is wrong from beginning to end. You can read about the truth of the matter in my books, especially in *Riddles of the Soul* and in various lecture courses. All I will do now is remind you that the human being consists of three members—the nerve-sense organism, that is, all that sustains the human being in the activity of its mind and spirit; the rhythmic organism, which contains the whole rhythm of breathing, the circulation of the blood, and so on; and the metabolic-limb organism, in which everything that is metamorphosed by various substances is to be found.

Now if you take the physical development of the child from birth to the change of teeth you will find it is specially the head-organization, the nerve-sense organization that is at work.[1] The child develops from the head downward in the

---

1. Dr. Steiner is here speaking of the process of organic development, not of the child's mental growth. There is no question of approaching the child's intellect during this first period of childhood when the head and nerves system is performing a function entirely different from later years. See Rudolf Steiner: *The Education of the Child in the Light of Anthroposophy.*

early years of life. You must examine this closely. Look first of all at a human embryo, an unborn child. The head is enormous and the rest of the body is still stunted. The child is born and the head is still outwardly the largest, strongest part, and out of the head proceeds the whole growth of the child.

This is no longer the case between the seventh and fourteenth year. Rhythm of breathing, rhythm of the blood, the whole rhythmic system is what holds sway between the change of teeth and puberty. Only rhythm!

But what is the real nature of rhythm? Now if you think a great deal, particularly if you have to study, you get tired, you get tired in your head. If you have to walk far, which is an exertion for the limb organism, you also tire. The head, or the nerve-sense organism, and the metabolic-limb organism can get tired. But the rhythmic organism can never tire.

For just think; you breathe all day long. Your heart beats at night as well as in the day. It must never stop, from birth to death. The rhythm of it has to go on all the time, and cannot ever tire. It never gets tired at all.

Now in education and teaching you must address yourself to whichever system is predominant in the child; thus between the change of teeth and puberty you must address yourself to rhythm in the child by using pictures. Everything that you describe or do must be done in such a way that the head has as little to do with it as possible, but the heart, the rhythm, everything that is artistic or rhythmic, must be engaged. What is the result? The result is that with teaching of this kind the child never gets tired, because you are engaging the rhythmic system, not the head.

People are very clever in this materialistic age, and so they have decided that children should always be allowed to romp about between lessons. Now it is certainly good to let them romp about, but it is good because of the soul qualities in it, because of the delight they have in it. For there have been experiments made that show when the children are properly taught in lesson time they are less tired than when they play about outside. The movement of their limbs tires them more, whereas what you give them in their lessons in the right way should never tire them at all. And the more you develop the pictorial element with the children and the less you exert the intellect, by presenting everything in a living way, the more you will be making demands on the rhythmic system only, and the less will the children become tired. Therefore when the experimental psychologists come and make observations to see how much the children tire, what is it they really observe? They observe how badly you have taught. If you had taught well they would find no fatigue on the part of the children.

In our work with children of elementary school age we must see to it that we engage the rhythmic system only. The rhythmic system never tires, and is not overexerted when we employ it in the right way, and for this rhythmic system we need not an intellectual but rather a pictorial method of presentation, something that comes out of the fantasy. Therefore it is imperative that fantasy should hold sway in the school. This must still be so even in the last period of which we have spoken, from eleven-and-two-thirds to fourteen years; we must still bring lifeless things to life through fantasy and always connect them with real life. It is possible to connect all the phenomena of physics with real life, but we ourselves must have fantasy in order to do it. This is absolutely necessary.

Now this fantasy should above all be the guiding principle in what are called compositions, when the children have to write about something and work it out for themselves. Here you must strictly avoid allowing the children to write a composition about anything that you have not first talked over with them. You yourself, with the authority of the teacher and educator, should have first spoken about the subject with the children; then the child should produce a composition under the influence of what you yourself have said. Even when the children are approaching puberty you must still not depart from this principle. Even then children should not just write whatever occurs to them; they should always feel that a certain mood has been aroused in them through having discussed the subject with their teacher, and all that they then write in their own essay must preserve this mood.

Here again it is "aliveness" that must be the guiding principle. "Aliveness" in the teacher must pass over to "aliveness" in the children.

As you will see from this, all of your teaching and education must be taken from real life. This is something you often hear nowadays. People say that lessons must be given in a living way and in accordance with reality. But first of all we must acquire a feeling for what is actually in accordance with reality. I will give you an example from my own experience of what sometimes happens in practice even when in theory people hold the most excellent educational principles.

I once went into a classroom where an arithmetic example was being given that was supposed to connect addition with real life. 14 2/3, 16 5/8 and 25 3/5 for example, were not simply to be added together, but were to be related to life. This was done in the following way: The children were told that one man was born on March 25, 1895, another on August 27, 1898, and a third on December 3, 1899. How old are these three men together? That was the question. And the sum was quite seriously carried through in the following way: from the given date in 1895 to 1924[2] is 29 3/4; this is the age of the first man. The second one up to 1924 is about 26 1/2 years old, and

---

2. The date of this lecture course.

the third, from 1899, as he was born on December 3, we may say 25. The children were then told that when they add up these ages they will find out how old they all are together.

But my dear friends, I should just like to ask how it is possible that they can make up a certain sum together with their ages? How do you set about it? Of course the numbers can quite well be made up into a sum, but where can you find such a sum in reality? The men are all living at the same time, so that they cannot possibly experience such a thing together in any way. A sum like this is not in the very least taken from life.

It was pointed out to me that this sum was actually taken from a book of examples. I then looked at this book and I found several other ingenious examples of the same kind. In many places I have found that this kind of thing has repercussions in ordinary life, and that is the important thing about it. For what we do at school affects ordinary life, and if the school teaching is wrong, that is if we bring such an unreality into an arithmetical example, then this way of thinking will be adopted by the young people and applied in ordinary life. I do not know if it is the same in England, but all over central Europe when, let us say, several criminals are accused and condemned together, you sometimes read in the papers: all five together have received sentences of imprisonment totalling 75 1/2 years. One has ten years, another twenty, and so on, but it is all added up together. You find this repeatedly in the newspapers. I would like to know what meaning a sum like that can have in reality. For each single prisoner who is sentenced, the 75 years together certainly have no meaning; they will all of them be free long before the 75 years are over, so it has no reality at all.

You see, what is the important thing is to make straight for the reality in everything: you simply poison a child to whom you give a sum that is absolutely impossible in real life.

relationship between "fantasy" and "reality"?

You must guide the child to think only about things that are to be found in life. Then through your teaching reality will be carried back into life again. In our time we suffer terribly from the unreality of people's thinking, and the teacher must consider this very carefully.

There is a theory today that, though postulated by people who are considered to be extraordinarily clever, is really only a product of education. It is the so-called Theory of Relativity. I hope you have already heard something of this theory that is connected with the name of Einstein; there is much in it that is correct, but it has been distorted in the following way. Let us imagine that a cannon is fired off somewhere. It is said that if you are so many miles away, after a certain length of time you hear the report of the cannon. If you do not stand still but walk away from the sound, then you hear it later. The quicker you walk away the later you get the impression of the sound. If you do the opposite and walk towards the sound you will be hearing it sooner and sooner all the time.

But now if you continue this thought you come to the possible conception, which is however an impossibility in reality, that you approach the sound more quickly than it travels itself, and then if you think this out to its conclusion you come to the point of saying to yourself: then there is also a possibility of hearing the sound before the cannon is fired off!

This is what it can lead to, if theories arise out of a kind of thinking that is not in accordance with reality. A person who can think in accordance with reality must sometimes have very painful experiences. In Einstein's books you even find, for instance, how you could take a watch and send it out into the universe at the speed of light, and then let it come back again; we are then told what happens to this watch if it goes out at the speed of light and comes back again. I should like to see the actual watch that, having whizzed away at this speed, then comes back again;

I should like to know what it looks like then! The essential thing
is that we never lose sight of reality in our thinking.

Herein lies the root of all evil in much of the education of
today, and you find, for instance, in the "exemplary" kindergartens that different kinds of work are thought out for the child
to do. In reality we should not allow the children to do anything, even in play, that is not an imitation of life itself. All
Froebel occupations and the like, which have been thought out
for the children, are really bad. We must make it a rule only to
let the children do what is an imitation of life, even in play.
This is extremely important.

For this reason, as I have already told you, we should not
provide what are called "ingenious" toys, but with dolls or
other toys we should leave as much as possible to the child's
own fantasy. This is of great significance, and I earnestly beg
you to make it a rule not to let anything come into your teaching and education that is not in some way connected with life.

The same rule applies when you ask the children to describe
something. You should always call their attention to it if they
stray from reality. The intellect never penetrates as deeply into
reality as fantasy does. Fantasy can go astray, it is true, but it is
rooted in reality, whereas the intellect remains always on the
surface. That is why it is so infinitely important for the teacher
to be in touch with reality as he or she stands in the class.

To support this we have our teachers' meetings in the Waldorf School, which are the heart and soul of the teaching. In
these meetings, all the teachers speak of what they as individuals have learned from their classes and from all the children in
them, so that each one learns from the other. No school is
really alive where this is not the most important thing, this regular meeting of the teachers.

And indeed there is an enormous amount one can learn
there. In the Waldorf School we have mixed classes, girls and

boys together. Now quite apart from what the boys and girls say to each other, or what they consciously exchange with each other, there is a marked difference to be seen in the classes according to whether there are more girls than boys or more boys than girls, or an equal number of each. For years I have been watching this, and it has always proved to be the case that there is something different in a class where there are more girls than boys.

In the latter case you will very soon find that you yourself as the teacher become less tired, because the girls grasp things more easily than boys and with greater eagerness too. You will find many other differences also. Above all, you will very soon discover that the boys themselves gain in quickness of comprehension when they are in a minority, whereas the girls lose by it if they are in the minority. And so there are numerous differences that do not arise through the way they talk together or treat each other but that remain in the sphere of the imponderable and are themselves imponderable things.

All these things must be very carefully watched, and everything that concerns either the whole class or individual children is spoken of in our meetings, so that every teacher really has the opportunity to gain an insight into characteristic individualities among the pupils.

There is one thing that is of course difficult in the Waldorf School method. We have to think much more carefully than is usually the case in class teaching, how one can really help the children progress. For we are striving to teach by "reading" from the particular age of a child what should be given at this age. All I have said to you is directed toward this goal.

Now suppose a teacher has a child of between nine and ten years in the class that is right for its age, but without much further thought the child is kept behind, and not allowed to go ahead with the rest of the class; the consequence will be that in the following year this child will be receiving teaching meant for children of a different age. Therefore under all circumstances we should avoid letting children stay behind in the same class even if they have not reached the required standard. This is not so convenient as letting the children stay in the class where they are and repeat the work, but we should avoid this at all costs. The only corrective we have is to put the very weak ones into a special class for the more backward children.[3]

Children who are in any way below standard come into this class from all the other classes.

Otherwise, as I have said, we do not let the children stay behind but we try to bring them along with us under all circumstances, so that in this way each child really receives what is right for his or her particular age.

We must also consider those children who have to leave school at puberty, at the end of the elementary school period, and who cannot therefore participate in the upper classes. We must make it our aim that by this time, through the whole tenor of our teaching, they will have come to a perception of the world that is in accordance with life itself. This can be done in a twofold way. On the one hand we can develop all our science and history lessons in a way that the children, at the end of their schooling, have some knowledge of the human being and some idea of the place of human beings in the world. Everything must lead up to a knowledge of the human being, reaching a measure of wholeness when the children come to the seventh and eighth grades, that is when they have reached their thirteenth and fourteenth year. Then all that they have already learned will enable them to understand what laws,

---

3. Dr. Steiner then added that these children were at that time being taught by Dr. Karl Schubert who had a very special task in this domain and was particularly gifted for it.

forces, and substances are at work in the human being itself, and how the human being is connected with all physical matter in the world, with all that is of soul in the world, and with all spirit in the world. Thus the children, in their own way of course, come to know what a human being is within the whole cosmos. This then is what we try to achieve on the one hand.

On the other hand, we try to give the children an understanding of life. It is actually the case today that most people, especially those who grow up in towns, have no idea how things, paper for instance, are made. There are a great many people who do not know how the paper on which they write or the material they are wearing is manufactured, nor, if they wear leather shoes, how the leather is prepared.

Think of how many people there are who drink beer and have no idea how the beer is made. This is really an unfortunate state of affairs. Now we cannot of course achieve everything in this regard, but we try to make it our aim as far as possible to give the children some knowledge of the work done in the various trades, and to see to it that they themselves also learn how to do different kinds of work that are done in real life.

It is, however, extraordinarily difficult, in view of what is demanded of children today by the authorities, to succeed with an education that is really related to life itself. One has to go through some very painful experiences. Once for instance, because of family circumstances, a child had to leave when he had just completed the second class and begun a new year in the third. He had to continue his education in another school. We were then most bitterly reproached because he had not got so far in arithmetic as was expected of him there, nor in reading or writing. Moreover they wrote and told us that the eurythmy and painting and all the other things he could do were of no use to him at all.

If, therefore, we want to educate the children not only out of knowledge of the human being, but also in accordance with the demands of life, they will need to know how to read and write properly when this is expected of them today. And so the curriculum will have to include many things simply because that is what is demanded by the customs of the time. Nevertheless, we must still try to relate the children to real life as much as possible.

I would dearly like to have a shoemaker as a teacher in the Waldorf School, if this were possible. It cannot be done because such a thing does not fit into a curriculum based on present-day requirements, but in order that the children might really learn to make shoes, and to know, not theoretically but through their own work, what this entails, I would dearly like to have a shoemaker on the staff of the school. But it simply cannot be done because it is not in accordance with the authorities, although it is just the very thing that is in accordance with real life. Nevertheless we do try to enable the children to be practical workers.

When you come to the Waldorf School you will see that the children are quite good at binding books and making boxes; you will see too how they are led into a really artistic approach to handwork; the girls will not be taught to produce the kind of thing you see today when you look at the clothes that women wear, for instance. It does not occur to people that the pattern for a collar should be different from that of a belt or the hem of a dress. People do not consider that here, for example, (see drawing a) the pattern must have a special character because it is worn at the neck. The pattern for a belt (see drawing b) must lead both upward and downward, and so on.

a

b

Or again, we never let our children make a cushion with an enclosed pattern, but the pattern itself should show where to lay your head. You can also see that there is a difference between right and left, and so forth. Thus here too life itself is woven and worked into everything that the children make, and they learn a great deal from it. This then is another method by which the children may learn to stand rightly in life.

We try to carry this out in every detail, for example in giving reports. I could never for the life of me imagine what it means to mark the capacities of the children with a 2, or 3, or 2 1/2. I do not know if this is done in England too, giving the children numbers or letters that are supposed to show what a child can do. In central Europe it is customary to give a 3, or a 4. At the Waldorf School we do not give reports like this, but every teacher knows every child and describes him or her in the report. The report describes in the teacher's own words what the child's capacities are and what progress the child has made.

And then every year each child receives in the report a personal motto or verse, which can be a word of guidance in the year to come. The report is like this: first there is the child's name and then the verse, and then the teacher—without using stereotyped letters or numbers—simply characterizes what the child is like, and what progress she or he has made in the different subjects. The report is thus a description. The children always love their reports, and their parents also get a true picture of what the child is like at school.

We lay great stress upon keeping in touch with the parents so that from the school we may see into the home through the child. Only in this way can we come to understand each child, and to know how to treat every peculiarity. For instance, we may notice a trait in one child that looks the same as a trait in another child; yet the meaning of that trait may be altogether different in the one case than in the other.

Suppose for instance that two children each show a certain excitability. It is not merely a question of knowing that the children are excitable and giving them something to help them quiet down. Rather, it is a question of finding out that one child has an excitable father who is being imitated, and that the other child is excitable because of a weak heart. In every case we must be able to discover what lies at the root of these peculiarities.

The real purpose of the teachers' meetings is to study the human being, so that a real knowledge of human beings is continually flowing through the school. The whole school is the concern of the teachers in their meetings, and all else that is needed will follow of itself. The essential thing is that in the teachers' meetings there is study—steady, continual study.

These are the indications I wanted to give you for the practical organization of your school.

There are of course many things that could still be said if we could continue this course for several weeks. But that we cannot do, and therefore I want to ask you tomorrow, when we come together, to put in the form of questions anything you may have upon your minds, so that we may use the time for you to ask your questions that I will then answer for you.

QUESTIONS AND ANSWERS
TORQUAY / AUGUST 20, 1924

What is the real difference between multiplication and division in this method of teaching? Or should there be no difference at all in the first school year?[1]

The question probably arises from my statement that in multiplication the so-called multiplicand (one factor) and the product are given, and the other factor has to be found. Of course this really gives what is usually regarded as division. If we do not keep too strictly to words, then on the same basis we can consider division, as follows:

We can say: If a whole is divided in a certain way, what is the amount of the part? And you have only another conception of the same thing as in the question: By what must a number be multiplied in order to get a certain other number?

Thus, if our question refers to dividing into parts, we have to do with a division: but if we regard it from the standpoint of "how many times…" then we are dealing with a multiplication. And it is precisely the inner relationship in thought that exists between multiplication and division that here appears most clearly.

But we should point out quite early on to the children that they can think of division in two ways. One is that which I have just indicated; here we examine how large each part is if we separate a whole into a definite number of parts. Here I proceed

---

1. The questions were handed to Dr. Steiner in writing.

from the whole to find the part; that is one kind of division. In the other kind of division I start from the part, and find out how often the part is contained in the whole: then the division is not a separation into parts, but a measurement. The child should be taught this difference between separation into parts and measurement as soon as possible, but without using pedantic terminology. Then division and multiplication will soon cease to be something in the nature of merely formal calculation, as it very often is, and will become connected with life.

So in the first school years it is really only in the method of expression that you can make a difference between multiplication and division; but you must be sure to point out that this difference is fundamentally much smaller than the difference between subtraction and addition. It is very important that the children should learn such things.

Thus we cannot say that no difference at all should be made between multiplication and division in the first school years, but it should be done in the way I have just indicated.

At what age and in what manner should we make the transition from the concrete to the abstract in arithmetic?

At first one should endeavor to keep entirely to the concrete in arithmetic, and above all avoid abstractions before the child comes to the turning point of the ninth and tenth years. Up to this time keep to the concrete as far as possible, by connecting everything directly with life.

When we have done that for two or two-and-one-half years and have really seen to it that calculations are not made with abstract numbers, but with concrete facts presented in the form of sums, then we shall see that the transition from the concrete to the abstract in arithmetic is extraordinarily easy. For in this method of dealing with numbers they become so alive in the child that one can easily pass on to the abstract treatment of addition, subtraction, and so on.

It will be a question, then, of postponing the transition from the concrete to the abstract, as far as possible, until the time between the ninth and tenth years of which I have spoken.

One thing that can help you in this transition from the abstract to the concrete is just that kind of arithmetic that one uses most in real life, namely the spending of money; and here you are more favorably placed than we are on the Continent, for there we have the decimal system for everything. Here, with your money, you still have a more pleasing system than this. I hope you find it so, because then you have a right and healthy feeling for it. The soundest, most healthy basis for a money system is that it should be as concrete as possible. Here you still count according to the twelve and twenty system which we have already "outgrown," as they say, on the Continent. I expect you already have the decimal system for measurement? (The answer was given that we do not use it for everyday purposes, but only in science.) Well, here too, you have the more pleasant system of measures! These are things that really keep everything to the concrete. Only in notation do you have the decimal system.

What is the basis of this decimal system? It is based on the fact that originally we had a natural measurement. I have told you that number is not formed by the head, but by the whole body. The head only reflects number, and it is natural that we should actually have ten, or twenty at the highest, as numbers. Now we have the number ten in particular, because we have ten fingers. The only numbers we write are from 1 to 10: after that we begin once more to treat the numbers themselves as concrete things.

Let us just write, for example: 2 donkeys. Here the donkey is the concrete thing, and the 2 is the number. I might just as well

say: 2 dogs. But if you write 20, that is nothing more than 2
times 10. Here the 10 is treated as a concrete thing. And so our
system of numeration rests upon the fact that when the thing
becomes too involved, and we no longer see it clearly, then we
begin to treat the number itself as something concrete, and
then make it abstract again. We should make no progress in
calculation unless we treated the number itself, no matter what
it is, as a concrete thing, and afterwards made it abstract. 100 is
really only 10 times 10. Now, whether I have 10 times 10, and
treat it as 100, or whether I have 10 times 10 dogs, it is really
the same. In one case the dogs, and in the other the 10 is the
concrete thing. The real secret of calculation is that the number
itself is treated as something concrete. And if you think this out
you will find that a transition also takes place in life itself. We
speak of 2 twelves—2 dozen—in exactly the same way as we
speak of 2 tens, only we have no alternative like "dozen" for the
ten because the decimal system has been conceived under the
influence of abstraction. All other systems still have much more
concrete conceptions of a quantity: a dozen: a shilling. How
much is a shilling? Here, in England, a shilling is 12 pennies.
But in my childhood we had a "shilling" that was divided into
30 units, but not monetary units. In the village where I lived
for a long time, there were houses along the village street on
both sides of the way. There were walnut trees everywhere in
front of the houses, and in the autumn the boys knocked down
the nuts and stored them for the winter. And when they came
to school they would boast about it. One would say: "I've got
five shillings already," and another: "I have ten shillings of
nuts." They were speaking of concrete things. A shilling always
meant 30 nuts. The farmers' only concern was to gather the
nuts early, before all the trees were already stripped! "A nut-shil-
ling" we used to say: that was a unit. To sell these nuts was a
right: it was done quite openly.

And so, by using these numbers with concrete things—one *dozen, two dozen, one pair, two pair, and so on.*, the transition from the concrete to the abstract can be made. We do not say: "four gloves," but: "Two pairs of gloves;" not: "Four shoes," but "two pairs of shoes." Using this method we can make the transition from concrete to abstract as a gradual preparation for the time between the ninth and tenth years when abstract number as such can be presented.[2]

When and how should drawing be taught?

With regard to the teaching of drawing, it is really a question of viewing the matter artistically. You must remember that drawing is a sort of untruth. What does drawing mean? It means representing something by lines, but in the real world there is no such thing as a line. In the real world there is, for example, the sea. It is represented by color (green); above it is the sky, also represented by color (blue). If these colors are brought together you have the sea below and the sky above (see sketch).

The line forms itself at the boundary between the two colors. To say that here (horizontal line) the sky is bounded by

---

2. It should be noted that before this transition from the concrete to the abstract dealt with above, a *rhythmic* approach is used in the teaching of the rudiments of number, e.g., the tables in the lower grades.

the sea is really a very abstract statement. So from the artistic point of view one feels that the reality should be represented in color, or else, if you like, in light and shade. What is actually there when I draw a face? Does such a thing as this really exist? (The outline of a face is drawn.) Is there anything of that sort? Nothing of the kind exists at all. What does exist is this: (see shaded drawing). There are certain surfaces in light and shade, and out of these a face appears. To bring lines into it, and form a face from them, is really an untruth: there is no such thing as this.

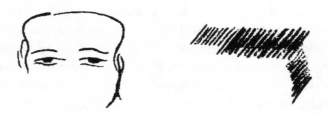

An artistic feeling will prompt you to work out what is really there out of black and white or color. Lines will then appear of themselves. Only when one traces the boundaries that arise in the light and shade or in the color do the "drawing lines" appear.

Therefore instruction in drawing must, in any case, not start from drawing itself but from painting, working in color or in light and shade. And the teaching of drawing, as such, is only of real value when it is carried out in full awareness that it gives us nothing real. A great amount of mischief has been wrought in our whole method of thinking by the importance attached to drawing. From this has arisen all that we find in optics, for example, where people are eternally drawing lines that are supposed to be rays of light. Where can we really find these rays of light? They are nowhere to be found. What you have in reality is pictures. You make a hole in a wall; the sun shines through it and on a screen an image is formed. The rays can perhaps be seen, if at all, in the particles of dust in the room—and the dustier the room, the more you can see of them. But what is usually drawn as lines in this connection is only imagined. Everything, really, that is drawn, has been thought out. And it is only when you begin to teach the child something like perspective, in which you already have to do with the abstract method of explanation, that you can begin to represent aligning and sighting by lines.

But the worst thing you can do is to teach the child to *draw* a horse or a dog with lines. He should take a paint brush and make a painting of the dog, but never a drawing. The outline of the dog does not exist at all: where is it? It is, of course, produced of itself if we put on paper what is really there.

We are now finding that not only children but also teachers would like to join our school. There may well be many teachers who would be glad to teach in the Waldorf School, because they would like it better there. I have had quite a number of people come to me recently and describe how they have been prepared for the teaching profession in the training colleges. The teachers of history, languages, and so on, are slightly shocking, but worst of all are the drawing teachers, for they are carrying on a craft that has no connection whatever with artistic feeling: such feeling simply does not exist.

And the result is (I am mentioning no names, so I can speak freely) that one can scarcely converse with the drawing teachers: they are such dried-up, such "un-human" people. They have no idea at all of reality. By taking up drawing as a profession they have lost touch with all reality. It is terrible to try to talk to them, quite apart from the fact that they want to teach drawing in the Waldorf School, where we have not introduced drawing at all. But the mentality of these people who carry on the unreal craft of drawing is also quite remarkable. And they have no moisture on the tongue—their tongues are quite dry. It is tragic to see what these drawing teachers gradually turn into, simply because of having to do something that is completely unreal.

I will therefore answer this question by saying that wherever possible you should start from painting and not from drawing. That is the important thing.

I will explain this matter more clearly, so that there will be no misunderstanding. You might otherwise think I had something personal against drawing teachers. I would like to put it thus: here is a group of children. I show them that the sun is shining in from this side. The sun falls upon something and makes all kinds of light (see sketch). Light is shed upon everything. I can see bright patches. It is because the sun is shining in that I can see the bright patches everywhere. But above them I see no bright patches, only darkness (blue). But I also see darkness here, below the bright patches: there will perhaps be just a little light here. Then I look at something that, when the light falls on it like this, looks greenish in color; and here, under the black shadow, it is also greenish, and there are other curious things to be seen in between the two. Here the light does not go right in.

You see, I have spoken of light and shadow, and of how there is something here on which the light does not impinge: and lo, I have made a tree! I have only spoken about light and color, and I have made a tree. We cannot really paint the tree: we can only bring in light and shade, and green, or a little yellow if you like, if the fruit happens to be lovely apples. But we must speak of color and light and shade; and so indeed we shall be speaking only of what is really there—color, light and shade. Drawing should only be done in geometry and all that is connected with it. There we have to do with lines, something that is worked out in thought. But realities, concrete realities must not be drawn with a pen; a tree, for example, must be evolved out of light and shade and out of the colors, for this is the reality of life itself.[3]

It would be barbarous if an orthodox drawing teacher came and had this tree, which we have drawn here in shaded color, copied in lines. In reality there are just light patches and dark patches. Nature does that. If lines were drawn here it would be an untruth.

---

3. The sketch was made on the blackboard with colored chalks but it has only been possible to reproduce it in black and white.

Should the direct method, without translation, be used, even for Latin and Greek?

In this respect a special exception must be made regarding Latin and Greek. It is not necessary to connect these directly with practical life, for they are no longer alive, and we have them only as dead languages. Now Greek and Latin (for Greek should actually precede Latin in teaching) can be taught only when the children are somewhat older, and therefore the translation method for these languages is, in a certain way, fully justified.

There is no question of our conversing in Latin and Greek. Our aim is to understand the ancient authors, and so we use these languages first and foremost for the purposes of translation. And thus we do not use the same methods for teaching Latin and Greek that we use with living languages.

Now once more comes the question that is put to me whenever I am anywhere in England where education is being discussed:

How should instruction in gymnastics be carried out, and should sports be taught in an English school, hockey and cricket, for example, and if so in what way?

It is emphatically not the aim of the Waldorf school method to suppress these things. They have their place simply because they play a great part in English life, and the children should grow up into life. Only please do not fall prey to the illusion that there is any other meaning in it than this, namely, that we ought not to make children strangers to their world. It is an error to believe that sports are of tremendous value in development. They are not of great value in development. Their only value is as a fashion dear to the English people, but we must not make the children strangers to the world by exclusion from all popular activities. You like sports in England, so the children should be introduced to sports. One should not meet with philistine opposition what may possibly be philistine itself.

Regarding "how it should really be taught," there is very little indeed to be said. For in these things it is really more or less so that the child imitates what someone does first. And to devise special artificial methods here would be something scarcely appropriate to the subject.

In drill or gymnastics one simply learns from anatomy and physiology in what position any limb of the organism must be placed to serve the agility of the body. It is a question of really having a sense for what makes the organism skilled, light and supple; and when one has this sense, one has then simply to demonstrate. Suppose you have a horizontal bar: it is customary to perform all kinds of exercises on the bar except the most valuable one of all, which consists in hanging on to the bar, hooked on, like this... then swinging sideways, and then grasping the bar further up, then swinging back, then grasping the bar again. There is no jumping but you hang from the bar, fly through the air, make the various movements, grasp the bar thus, and thus, and so an alternation in the shape and position of the muscles of the arms is produced that actually has a healthy effect upon the whole body.

You must study which inner movements of the muscles have a healthy effect on the organism, so that you will know what movements to teach. Then you have only to do the exercises in front of the children, for the method consists simply in this preliminary demonstration.[4]

---

4. A method of gymnastic teaching on the lines indicated above was subsequently worked out by Fritz Graf Bothmer, teacher of gymnastics at the Waldorf School, Stuttgart.

How should religious instruction be given at the different ages?

As I always speak from the standpoint of practical life, I have to say that the Waldorf School method is a method of education and is not meant to bring into the school a philosophy of life or anything sectarian. Therefore I can only speak of what lives within the Waldorf School principle itself.

It was comparatively easy for us in Württemberg, where the laws of education were still quite liberal: when the Waldorf School was established we were really shown great consideration by the authorities. It was even possible for me to insist that I myself should appoint the teachers without regard to their having passed any state examination or not. I do not mean that everyone who has passed a state examination is unsuitable as a teacher! I would not say that. But still, I could see nothing in a state examination that would necessarily qualify a person to become a teacher in the Waldorf School.

And in this respect things have really always gone quite well. But one thing was necessary when we were establishing the school, and that was for us definitely to take this standpoint: We have a "method-school"; we do not interfere with social life as it is at present, but through anthroposophy we find the best method of teaching, and the school is purely a "method-school."

Therefore, I arranged from the outset that religious instruction should not be included in our school syllabus, but that Catholic religious teaching should be delegated to the Catholic priest, and the Protestant teaching to the pastor and so on.

In the first few years most of our scholars came from a factory (the Waldorf-Astoria cigarette factory), and among them we have many "dissenting" children, children whose parents were of no religion. But our educational conscience of course demanded that a certain kind of religious instruction should be given them also. We therefore arranged a "free religious teaching" for these children, and for this we have a special method.

In these "free religion lessons" we first of all teach gratitude in the contemplation of everything in nature. Whereas in the telling of legends and myths we simply relate what things do—stones, plants, and so on—here in the religion lessons we lead the children to perceive the Divine in all things. So we begin with a kind of "religious naturalism," shall I say, in a form suited to the children.

Again, the children cannot be brought to an *understanding* of the Gospels before the time between the ninth and tenth years of which I have spoken. Only then can we proceed to a consideration of the Gospels in the religion lessons, going on later to the Old Testament. Up to this time we can only introduce the children to a kind of nature-religion in its general aspect, and for this we have our own method. Then we should go on to the Gospels but not before the ninth or tenth year, and only much later, between the twelfth and thirteenth years, should we proceed to the Old Testament.[5]

This then is how you should think of the free religion lessons. We are not concerned with the Catholic and Protestant

---

5. This paragraph can easily be misunderstood unless two other aspects of the education are kept in mind. Firstly: Here Dr. Steiner is only speaking of the content of the actual religion lessons. In the class teaching all children are introduced to the stories of the Old Testament. Secondly, quite apart from the religion lessons the festivals of the year are celebrated with all children in a Rudolf Steiner school, in forms adapted to their ages. Christmas takes a very special place, and is prepared for throughout Advent by carol singing, the daily opening of a star-window in the "Advent calendar" and the lighting of candles on the Advent wreath hung in the classroom. At the end of the Christmas term the teachers perform traditional nativity plays as their gift to the children. All this is in the nature of an *experience* for the children, inspired by feeling and the Christmas mood. Later, in the religion lessons, on the basis of this experience, they can be brought to a more conscious knowledge and understanding of the Gospels.

instruction: we must leave that to the Catholic and Protestant pastors. Also every Sunday we have a special form of service for those who attend the free religion lessons. A service is performed and forms of worship are provided for children of different ages. What is done at these services has shown its results in practical life during the course of the years; it contributes in a very special way to the deepening of religious feeling, and awakens a mood of great devotion in the hearts of the children.

We allow the parents to attend these services, and it has become evident that this free religious teaching truly brings new life to Christianity. And there is real Christianity in the Waldorf School, because through this naturalistic religion during the early years the children are gradually led to an understanding of the Christ Mystery, when they reach the higher classes.

Our free religion classes have, indeed, gradually become full to overflowing. We have all kinds of children coming into them from the Protestant pastor or the Catholic priest, but we make no propaganda for it. It is difficult to find sufficient religion teachers, and therefore it is a great burden when many children come; neither do we wish the school to acquire the reputation of being an anthroposophical school of a sectarian kind. We do not want that at all. Only our educational conscience has constrained us to introduce this free religion teaching. But children turn away from the Catholic and Protestant teaching and more and more come over to us and want to have the free religion teaching: they like it better. It is not our fault that they leave their other teachers: but as I have said, the principle of the whole thing was that religious instruction should be given, to begin with, by the various pastors. When you ask, then, what kind of religious teaching we have, I can only speak of what our own free religion teaching is, as I have just described it.

*Should French and German be taught from the beginning in an
English school? If the children come to a kindergarten class at five
or six years old, should they also have language lessons?*

As to whether French and German should be taught from
the beginning in an English school, I should first like to say
that I think this must be settled entirely on grounds of expedi-
ency. If you simply find that life makes it necessary to teach
these languages, you must teach them. We have introduced
French and English into the Waldorf School, because with
French there is much to be learned from the inner quality of
the language not found elsewhere, namely, a certain feeling for
rhetoric, which it is very good to acquire: and English is
taught because it is a universal world language, and will
become so more and more.

Now, I would not wish to decide categorically whether
French and German should be taught in an English school,
but you must be guided by the circumstances of life. It is not
at all so important which language is chosen as that foreign
languages are actually taught in the school.

And if children of four or five years do already come to
school (which should not really be the case) it would then be
good to do languages with them also. It would be right for
this age. Some kind of language teaching can be given even
before the age of the change of teeth, but it should only be
taught as a proper lesson after this change. If you have a kindergarten class for the little children, it would be quite right
to include the teaching of languages but all other school subjects should be postponed as far as possible until after the
change of teeth.

. . . . .

I would like to express, in conclusion, what you will readily appreciate, namely, that I am deeply gratified that you are taking such an active interest in making the Waldorf School method fruitful here in England, and that you are working with such energy for the establishment of a school here based on anthroposophy. And I should like to express the hope that you may succeed in making use of what you were able to learn from our training courses in Stuttgart, from what you have heard at various other courses in England, and finally, from what I have been able to give you here in a more aphoristic way, in order to establish a really good school here on anthroposophical lines. You must remember how much depends upon the success of the first attempt. If it does not succeed, a great deal is lost, for all else will be judged by the first attempt. And indeed, very much depends on how your first project is launched: from it the world must take notice that the initiative is neither something that is steeped in abstract, dilettante plans of school reform, nor anything amateur, but something that arises out of a conception of the real being of humanity, and is now to be brought to bear on the art of education. And it is indeed the very civilization of today, which is now moving through such critical times, that calls us to undertake this task, along with many others.

In conclusion I should like to give you my best thoughts on your path—the path that is to lead to the founding of a school here based on Anthroposophy.

THE FOUNDATIONS
OF WALDORF EDUCATION

THE FIRST FREE WALDORF SCHOOL opened its doors in Stuttgart, Germany, in September, 1919, under the auspices of Emil Molt, the Director of the Waldorf Astoria Cigarette Company and a student of Rudolf Steiner's spiritual science and particularly of Steiner's call for social renewal.

It was only the previous year—amid the social chaos following the end of World War I—that Emil Molt, responding to Steiner's prognosis that truly human change would not be possible unless a sufficient number of people received an education that developed the whole human being, decided to create a school for his workers' children. Conversations with the minister of education and with Rudolf Steiner, in early 1919, then led rapidly to the forming of the first school.

Since that time, more than six hundred schools have opened around the globe—from Italy, France, Portugal, Spain, Holland, Belgium, Great Britain, Norway, Finland, and Sweden to Russia, Georgia, Poland, Hungary, Romania, Israel, South Africa, Australia, Brazil, Chile, Peru, Argentina, Japan, and others—making the Waldorf school movement the largest independent school movement in the world. The United States, Canada, and Mexico alone now have more than 120 schools.

Although each Waldorf school is independent, and although there is a healthy oral tradition going back to the first Waldorf teachers and to Steiner himself, as well as a growing body of secondary literature, the true foundations of the Waldorf method and spirit remain the many lectures that Rudolf Steiner gave on the subject. For five years (1919–24), Rudolf Steiner, while simultaneously working on many other fronts, tirelessly dedicated himself to the dissemination of the idea of Waldorf education. He gave manifold lectures to teachers, parents, the general public, and even the children themselves. New schools were founded. The movement grew.

While many of Steiner's foundational lectures have been translated and published in the past, some have never appeared in English, and many have been virtually unobtainable for years. To remedy this situation and to establish a coherent basis for Waldorf education, Anthroposophic Press has decided to publish the complete series of Steiner lectures and writings on education in a uniform series. This series will thus constitute an authoritative foundation for work in educational renewal, for Waldorf teachers, parents, and educators generally.

RUDOLF STEINER'S LECTURES
(AND WRITINGS) ON EDUCATION

I. *Allgemeine Menschenkunde als Grundlage der Pädagogik. Pedagogischer Grundkurs,* 14 Lectures Stuttgart, 1919 (GA 293). Previously *The Study of Man. The Foundations of Human Experience* (Anthroposophic Press, 1996.)

II. *Erziehungskunst Methodische-Didaktisches,* 14 Lectures, Stuttgart, 1919 (GA 294). *Practical Advice to Teachers* (Anthroposophic Press, 2000).

III. *Erziehungskunst,* 15 Discussions, Stuttgart, 1919 (GA 295). *Discussions with Teachers* (Anthroposophic Press Press, 1997).

IV. *Die Erziehungsfrage als soziale Frage,* 6 Lectures, Dornach, 1919 (GA 296). Previously *Education as a Social Problem. Education as a Force for Social Change* (Anthroposophic Press, 1997).

V. *Die Waldorf Schule und ihr Geist,* 6 Lectures, Stuttgart and Basel, 1919 (GA 297). *The Spirit of the Waldorf School* (Anthroposophic Press, 1995).

VI. *Rudolf Steiner in der Waldorfschule, Vorträge und Ansprachen,* Stuttgart, 1919–1924 (GA 298). *Rudolf Steiner in the Waldorf School: Lectures and Conversations* (Anthroposophic Press, 1996).

VII. *Geisteswissenschaftliche Sprachbetrachtungen,* 6 Lectures, Stuttgart, 1919 (GA 299). *The Genius of Language* (Anthroposophic Press, 1995).

VIII. *Konferenzen mit den Lehren der Freien Waldorfschule 1919–1924,* 3 Volumes (GA 300a-c). *Faculty Meetings with Rudolf Steiner, 2 Volumes* (Anthroposophic Press, 1998).

IX. *Die Erneuerung der Pädagogisch-didaktischen Kunst durch Geisteswissenschaft,* 14 Lectures, Basel, 1920 (GA 301). *The Renewal of Education* (Anthroposophic Press, 2001).

X. *Menschenerkenntnis und Unterrichtsgestaltung,* 8 Lectures, Stuttgart, 1921 (GA 302). Previously *The Supplementary Course— Upper School* and *Waldorf Education for Adolescence. Education for Adolescents* (Anthroposophic Press, 1996).

XI. *Erziehung und Unterrricht aus Menschenerkenntnis,* 9 Lectures, Stuttgart, 1920, 1922, 1923 (GA 302a). *Balance in Teaching* (Anthroposophic Press, 2007).

XII. *Die Gesunder Entwickelung des Menschenwesens,* 16 Lectures, Dornach, 1921–22 (GA 303). *Soul Economy: Body, Soul, and Spirit in Waldorf Education* (Anthroposophic Press, 2003).

XIII. *Erziehungs- und Unterrichtsmethoden auf Anthroposophische Grundlage,* 9 Public Lectures, various cities, 1921–22 (GA304). *Waldorf Education and Anthroposophy I* (Anthroposophic Press, 1995).

XIV. *Anthroposophische Menschenkunde und Pädagogik,* 9 Public L and *Anthroposophy II* (Anthroposophic Press, 1995).

XV. *Die geistig-seelischen Grundkräfte der Erziehungskunst,* 12 Lectures, 1 Special Lecture, Oxford 1922 (GA 305) *The Spiritual Ground of Education* (Anthroposophic Press, 2004).

XVI. *Die pädagogisch Praxis vom Gesichtspunkte geisteswissenschaftliche Menschenerkenntnis,* 8 Lectures, Dornach, 1923 (GA 306). *The Child's Changing Consciousness and Waldorf Education* (Anthroposophic Press, 1996).

XVII. *Gegenwärtiges Geistesleben und Erziehung,* 4 Lectures, 1923 (GA 307). *A Modern Art of Education* (Anthroposophic Press, 2004) and *Education and Modern Spiritual Life* (Garber Publications, 1989).

XVIII. *Die Methodik des Lehrens und die Lebensbedingungen des Erziehens,* 5 Lectures, Stuttgart, 1924 (GA 308). *The Essentials of Education* (Anthroposophic Press, 1997).

XIX. *Anthroposophische Pädagogik und ihre Voraussentzungen,* 5 Lectures, Bern, 1924 (GA 309). *The Roots of Education* (Anthroposophic Press, 1997).

XX. *Der pädagogische Wert der Menschenerkenntnis und der Kultur-wert der Pädagogik,* 10 Public Lectures, Arnheim, 1924 (GA 310). *Human Values in Education* (Anthroposophic Press, 2005).

XXI. *Die Kunst des Erziehens aus dem Erfassen der Menschenwe-senheit,* 7 Lectures, Torquay, 1924 (GA 311). *The Kingdom of Childhood* (Anthroposophic Press, 1995).

XXII. *Geisteswissenschaftliche Impulse zur Entwicklung der Physik. Erster naturwissenschaftliche Kurs: Licht, Farbe, Ton—Masse, Elektrizität, Magnetismus,* 10 Lectures, Stuttgart, 1919–20 (GA 320). *The Light Course* (Anthroposophic Press, 2001).

XXIII. *Geisteswissenschaftliche Impulse zur Entwickelung der Physik. Zweiter naturwissenschaftliche Kurs: die Wärme auf die Grenze positiver und negativer Materialität,* 14 Lectures, Stuttgart, 1920 (GA 321). *The Warmth Course* (Mercury Press, 1988).

XXIV. *Das Verhältnis der verschiedenen naturwissenschaftlichen Gebiete zur Astronomie. Dritter naturwissenschaftliche Kurs: Himmelskunde in Bezeiehung zum Menschen und zur Menschenkunde,* 18 Lectures, Stuttgart, 1921 (GA 323). Available in typescript only as "**The Relation of the Diverse Branches of Natural Science to Astronomy.**"

XXV. *The Education of the Child and Early Lectures on Education* (A collection) (Anthroposophic Press, 1996).

XXVI. Miscellaneous.

INDEX

A

abstraction
avoidance of in classroom, 72-73, 78, 84, 106-107, 112
language as, 102
transition from to concrete, 126-129
See also materialism

actions
effect of on inner child, 17-19
relation of to space, 106-108
relation of to thinking, 69-70, 104
representation of among objects, 31
See also karma; movement

adults, 5, 8-9, 20
conduct of affecting child, 17-19
effect on of childhood experiences, 6, 17, 27, 31-32, 70, 73, 84
See also parents

age groups
development demands of, 50
differences between, 7
in relation to student advancement, 119-120
See also change of teeth

agriculture, 40, 48-49

alphabet, pictorial representation of, 24-26

animals
expression of will by, 106
human characteristics embodied in, 42-50
representation of to children, 31, 36, 37, 42-43, 50, 109
See also dogs

animism, childhood spirituality confused for, 30-31

anthropomorphism, representation of world using, 31, 36

Anthroposophy, as basis for education, 1, 3-4, 27, 33, 57

arithmetic
as punishment, 52-53
teaching of, 15, 71, 76, 78-81, 84, 115, 121, 125-129
See also counting

artistic sense development
in child, 23-24, 92, 129-133
in teacher, 15, 32, 33, 49, 50, 98-100, 109

astral body
activity of, 94-95
relation of to learning, 54-55
See also body; etheric body

atom
as demonic caricature, 79
See also whole

authority
maintenance of in classroom, 34-35, 61, 73, 98, 114
requirements of affecting curriculum, 122
See also discipline; punishment

autonomy. *See* independence

B

bad
contrasted with good, 65

counting
  teaching of, 72-79, 84-85, 127
  See also arithmetic
courage, 42, 44
  required for teachers, 56, 57
cows, 97-98, 104
cruelty, 42
cultural life, 1, 4
  effect on of materialism, 78-79
curiosity
  compared to spiritual longing,
    12-13
  evolution of, 13-14
  See also fantasy; imagination

D
dance. *See* eurythmy; movement
death
  perception of by child, 110
  preservation of language after,
    104-105
dexterity, development of, 21, 77
digestive process, 97-98
discipline
  maintenance of in classroom, 60
  See also authority
division, teaching of, 125-126
dogs, 31, 46-47, 60-61, 74, 75,
    105, 128
  See also animals
dolls, 22, 118
drawing
  classroom exercises for, 66-67
  teaching of, 129-133

E
earth
  as living being, 39, 40-41, 48,
    110
  relation of animals to, 42
  relation of with plants, 38, 39,
    40, 41, 42, 48-50

earthly life
  educational preparation for, 49
  spiritual descent into, 2, 12, 42
  See also environment; nature;
    pre-earthly life
eating, experience of by child, 19-
    20
education
  Anthroposophical basis for, 1, 5,
    7, 27, 50, 57, 113, 115
  kindergarten education weak-
    nesses, 18-19
  See also teaching
educational reform, 2, 5
ego
  as component of human being,
    94
  development of, 30, 33-34
  differentiation of within child,
    48, 109
  See also individuality
emotions
  distinguishing from knowledge,
    2
  effect of upon young child, 17-
    19
  expression of in story-telling,
    31-32
  See also feelings
environment
  adaptation of child to, 8
  differentiation of child from,
    33-34, 36, 48, 99, 104, 109
  disinterest of child in, 12-13, 14
  earth forces within, 38
  relation of child to, 12, 16-23,
    30-31
etheric body
  activity of, 17, 42, 92, 94
  See also astral body; body
eurythmy, 20, 121
  compared to sports, 106-107

pictures
  higher knowledge received as,
    41-42, 62, 96-97
  as language of children,
    32-33, 51-52, 56-57, 63, 66,
    131
  perception of, 17, 23
  See also stories
plants
  relation of with earth, 37-42,
    48-50, 111
  representation of to children,
    31, 36, 37-42, 48, 50,
    109
"practical" people
  harm done by, 4-5
  isolate nature of, 40
  See also materialism
pre-earthly life
  descent from into earthly life, 2,
    12-13, 42, 104
  expression of in child, 7-9
  See also life
previous lives
  characteristics of revealed by
    walking, 21
  characteristics of revealed in
    head, 76
  resolution of, 9
  See also incarnation;
    karma
puberty
  astral body activity in, 94
  "spiritual milk" provisions for,
    15
  teaching methods during, 16,
    115, 120
public life, preparation of child
  for, 27
punishment
  at Waldorf School, 52-53
  See also naughtiness

Q
questions
  allowance of time for, 60-61
  See also stories

R
reading
  harm resulting from early teach-
    ing of, 26, 119
  relation of to writing, 15, 26-27
  teaching of, 25, 71, 104, 121-
    122
  See also writing
reality
  pictures as, 26
  representation of to child, 37-
    42, 118, 122
reasoning powers, 14
  See also intellection
religious instruction, 65-66
  in relation to age groups, 136-
    138
reports, procedures for, 123-124
rhythmic system, 113-114
rock
  living origins of, 41
  See also stone

S
sanguines, seating of by tempera-
    ment, 63, 64
second body, formation of, 10-
    11, 16, 91-92
self. *See* ego
self-confidence, required of
    teacher, 62
self-knowledge, required of
    teacher, 54
sense-organ
  perception of pictures by, 23
  young child as, 16-23
shame, as disciplinary tool, 53

DURING THE LAST TWO DECADES of the nineteenth century the Austrian-born Rudolf Steiner (1861–1925) became a respected and well-published scientific, literary, and philosophical scholar, particularly known for his work on Goethe's scientific writings. After the turn of the century he began to develop his earlier philosophical principles into an approach to methodical research of psychological and spiritual phenomena.

His multifaceted genius has led to innovative and holistic approaches in medicine, science, education (Waldorf schools), special education, philosophy, religion, economics, agriculture (Biodynamic method), architecture, drama, new arts of eurythmy and speech, and other fields. In 1924 he founded the General Anthroposophical Society, which today has branches throughout the world.

Look up / listen to podcasts:
  - Waldorf 1st, 2nd, 3rd, 4th grade

Look up:
  - Elementary teacher interview questions

9 780880 104029